Beyond B
24 More Country Walks

Robin Tetlow

Publisher's note
At the time of publication, all routes were carefully checked and followed public rights of way.
Whilst every care has been taken to ensure the accuracy of the route description, the
publishers and author accept no responsibility for errors, omissions, or inaccuracies – or for
any loss or injury that could result. Any walks undertaken are entirely at your own risk.
The maps are for illustrative purposes only and are not to scale.

First published in 2019 by Redcliffe Press Ltd.,
81g Pembroke Road, Bristol BS8 3EA
Reprinted March 2021

info@redcliffepress.co.uk
www.redcliffepress.co.uk   @RedcliffePress   redcliffepress

© Robin Tetlow: text and photographs; cover painting: Lara Tetlow; cover design: Stephen Morris
The maps used in this book are reproduced by permission of Ordnance Survey ©Crown Copyright
2019 OS Licence 100058353. The maps are included for illustrative purposes only and are not
reproduced to scale.

ISBN 978-1-911408-41-3

British Library Cataloguing-in-Publication Data
A catalogue record for this book is available from the British Library

All rights reserved. Except for the purpose of review, no part of this book may be reproduced,
stored in a retrieval system, or transmitted, in any form or by any means, electronic, mechanical,
photocopying, recording or otherwise, without the prior permission of the publishers.

Design and typesetting by Stephen Morris www.stephen-morris.co.uk Set in Goudy 10/12
Printed and bound in the Czech Republic via Akcent Media

Redcliffe Press Ltd is committed to being an environmentally friendly publisher.
This book is made from Forest Stewardship Council® certified paper.

The Walks

	page
1 Old Sodbury, Little Sodbury and Horton – 8 miles / 13 kms	8
2 Stone, Ham and Whitcliff Park – 6 miles / 9.5 kms	14
3 Cheddar Gorge – 7.5 miles / 12 kms	19
4 Tintern and Brockweir – 6.75 miles / 10.5 kms	24
5 Aust, Littleton and Oldbury – 10 miles / 16 kms	29
6 Brent Knoll and Berrow Sands – 11 miles / 18 kms	34
7 Queen Charlton, Keynsham and Compton Dando – 8.5 miles / 14 kms	39
8 Burrington Combe, Velvet Bottom and Beacon Batch – 10.5 miles / 17 kms	44
9 Fretherne, Arlingham and Saul – 10.5 miles / 17 kms	49
10 Shirenewton, Llanmelin Fort and Itton Common – 8 miles / 13 kms	56
11 Newnham, Blaize Bailey and Bullo – 10 miles / 16 kms	62
12 Luckington, Littleton Drew and Alderton – 8 miles / 13 kms	68
13 Blagdon, Ubley and Butcombe – 7.25 miles / 11.5 kms	73
14 Congresbury, Cleeve and Wrington – 8.5 miles / 14 kms	79
15 Cold Ashton, Langridge and Lansdown – 10 miles / 16 kms	85
16 Box and Box Hill – 8 miles / 13 kms	91
17 Sherston and Easton Grey – 7.5 miles / 12 kms	97
18 Kellaways, Bremhill and East Tytherton – 8.5 miles / 14 kms	104
19 Nailsworth, Kingscote and Horsley – 9 miles / 14.5 kms	110
20 Wellow, Faulkland and Norton St Philip – 11 miles / 18 kms	116
21 Wedmore, Rodney Stoke and Nyland Hill – 9 miles / 15 kms	122
22 Wells, Croscombe and Dinder – 7.5 miles / 12 kms	127
23 Coaley Peak, Selsley Common and Woodchester Park – 8.5 miles / 14 kms	132
24 Chew Magna, Stanford Drew and Pensford – 10.5 miles / 17 kms	137

Why *Beyond Bristol 2?*

As well as attracting ever increasing numbers of tourists and visitors, greater Bristol is an increasingly desirable and fashionable region in which to live and work. Perhaps one of the more underestimated of the many assets of the area, is its easy access to countryside of outstanding quality and diversity.

The Mendips, the Cotswolds, the Somerset Levels, the Severn Estuary, the Wye Valley and the Forest of Dean are all within easy range... but there is so much more. There are numerous facets to explore, all within easy range of Bristol – including flora, fauna, woodland, coastline, rivers, canals, lakes, parkland, villages, market towns, ancient forts, castles, monuments, churches, country houses, historic buildings and ruins, burial mounds, industrial archaeology...

The response to *Beyond Bristol: 24 Country Walks* has far exceeded my initial expectations – both the sales of the book and more especially the positive feedback from readers telling me how much they have enjoyed the walks.

I started out on the first volume with the objective of featuring my 24 all-time favourites, drawn from more than 300 different walks I reckon to have done in the area over the past 30 plus years. In preparing this second volume, I have sought to identify 24 more favourites, each completely different yet of a similar quality to those in the first book. None of these further walks would have been out of place in the first volume. Indeed, I have found myself frequently wondering why most of them did not make the original selection!

The purpose and principles of volume 2 – the intended audience, the framework for the walks and the format – remain very much the same. My aim continues to be to guide you towards enjoying the best of the outstanding countryside beyond Bristol, throughout the changing seasons.

Are these walks for you?

All the walks are within easy reach of Bristol, all are serious walks, and all should be within the capabilities of most people. The book is targeted at the following overlapping audiences:

● If you are looking to get fitter and healthier, this book aims to prove to you that a half- or a full-day foray into the countryside is the ideal escape from stressful everyday life. Walking is both healthy and enjoyable. The physical and mental benefits of regular walking are becoming increasingly recognised.

● If you have never fully explored the countryside beyond Bristol before, this is your opportunity to discover what you have been missing. You may be a longstanding resident; or you may have only recently moved to the area; or you may simply be visiting.

● If you are an active walker already familiar with the countryside beyond Bristol, this book will hopefully still be a helpful compilation of some of the best walks – avoiding the need to plan your own routes or at least assisting you in doing so.

How have I chosen the 24 walks?
The selection is inevitably subjective. However, each of the walks does fit within the following broad framework:
- All the walks are easily accessible from the centre of Bristol – that is no more than 30 to 35 miles or one hour away by car.
- The length of each of the walks is within the range of 6 miles to 11 miles. The length is intended to be sufficient to justify a special trip to the start and to ensure some serious exercise. Similarly, the achievable time for each of the walks is in the range of 3 hours to 6 hours.
- As far as possible, the walks traverse the highest quality landscapes, and incorporate features of historical, archaeological and natural interest. As far as possible, as country walks, they avoid busy roads and other noisy distractions.
- I have aimed to select a representative range and variety of walks across the whole of area.
- I continue to acknowledge the inspiration and influence of other, mostly out-of-print publications produced over the past 30 plus years.

How the information on the 24 walks is formatted and presented
Please note the following about the format of the book and the guidance given for each of the 24 walks:
- Comprehensive written instructions are given for each of the walks. I have done each of them many times and at different times of the year. However, conditions vary greatly through the seasons – for example, conditions underfoot will tend to be muddier between November and March.
- The text for each walk explains the route in detail and is complemented by an OS extract showing the route and some key stages along it. Please note, however, that these maps are not reproduced to their original scale. Therefore, it may be advisable to carry with you the identified OS Explorer 1:25.000 map.
- Estimated distances are provided. The total walk lengths have been checked on Plotaroute. Shorter distances on the walks are in metric only.
- Estimated walking times have been provided for each walk. Of course, your actual time will depend not only on the conditions and your pace but also on how frequently you choose to stop to view the various features and/or for refreshments.
- This is first and foremost a walking book. The emphasis is on ensuring that you find your way round the route. The description of the features and scenery is economical. So, whilst most of the walks incorporate features of special natural, historical or archaeological interest, I often simply point them out without much detail. It is easy to delve further if you want.
- Car parking suggestions are made for each of the walks. For some, there is generous dedicated car parking at or near to the start; for others, the options are more limited, and you may have to look beyond the immediate locations I have suggested. Please always park sensibly and considerately.

• Some of the walks are accessible by public transport and I would encourage this option if available. However, in view of all the variables it is only realistic to leave you to do your own investigations.
• Refreshment options are listed for each of the walks. Neither their availability nor their quality have influenced the selection of the walks. I strongly suggest that you check all the relevant details, such as opening times, in advance; especially as the long-term future of a couple of the pubs mentioned appears doubtful.
• I have done my best to provide up to date and accurate information on each of the routes. I have carefully checked each of the routes in the very recent past. My checks have confirmed, though, that changes will inevitably continue to occur from time to time. Fortunately, most should be minor, such as gates replacing stiles. Apologies in advance, if I have not been as clear as I should.
• This book is designed to enable you to escape from the stresses of modern technology, so it does not specifically cater for following the routes via your mobile phone.
• All these walks are suitable for many occasions, at different times of the year and in a range of different conditions. Above all, it is for you to enjoy the various features of these walks in your own way.

Additional practical advice
I offer the following further additional advice, based on my experience of completing each of these walks on many occasions:
• Be realistic about your fitness and capabilities. There are a range of walks in this book; ultimately all should be within the capabilities of anyone who is reasonably fit and active. However, if you have not done much walking before you may need to build up your fitness first by doing some training walks in your locality. Otherwise you could start with some of the shorter and gentler walks in the book and progress from there.
• Wear stout shoes/ankle-high walking boots with socks for all walks in all conditions. Protect your legs – I would not recommend shorts even in the hottest of conditions. Avoid jeans, especially in wet conditions.

- Walking poles are very helpful, particularly on those walks including steeper gradients. I now take a single walking pole with me on every walk - they can have other uses, such as in clearing away brambles.
- Be mindful of the recent weather, for example the amount of rainfall will affect conditions underfoot and may affect your choice of walk.
- Check the weather forecast the day before and on the day of the walk; and take account of anticipated conditions in your preparation.
- Take a rucksack. Regardless of conditions and intended refreshment stops, it will always be sensible to carry with you your mobile phone (for emergency use), some food, some drink (about a litre) and plasters; and to have in reserve waterproofs, gloves and layers of clothing.

Please observe the Countryside Code

Please ensure that you keep to the Natural England Countryside Code but expect others to do so as well. See:
www.gov.uk/government/publications/the-countryside-code
The key elements for walkers are:
- Be safe, plan ahead and follow any signs.
- Leave gates open or closed as you find them, and use gates, stiles or gaps when they are provided; do not climb over gates or fences unless necessary.
- Protect plants and animals and take your litter home.
- Keep dogs under close control.
- Consider others.

Please join the Ramblers Association

I trust that you will enjoy completing, and regularly repeating, these walks as much I have. If you do, then please ensure you join the Ramblers Association, which I have belonged to myself for more than 40 years. This national organisation exists to promote the interests of walkers and walking, particularly in maintaining and improving footpaths. On many of the routes you will see that the organisation has directly contributed to waymarking and to the provision of new gates and stiles. Local groups, of which there are several in the Bristol area, organise regular walks. See **www.ramblers.org.uk**

Acknowledgements

I gratefully acknowledge the continued support and encouragement of Clara Hudson of Redcliffe Press Ltd, who has overseen the whole publication process; and of Stephen Morris, who has co-ordinated the design, layout and typesetting. As with the first volume, it has been, very much, a team effort.

Last but, most certainly not least, I thank my immediate family, Dina, Lara and Justin for their help and inspiration throughout. Particular thanks are due to Lara for the cover painting.

Robin Tetlow, September 2019

No. 1
Old Sodbury, Little Sodbury and Horton

Distance 8 miles / 13 kms
Time 4 hours
OS Map Explorer 167
Starting Point Outside the Dog Inn, Chapel Lane, Old Sodbury – OS reference 753816
Parking Free on-street parking at the northern end of Chapel Lane, towards the Dog Inn
Reaching the start from Bristol Go east on the M4. Leave by Junction 18 and then go north on the A46. At the traffic lights at Old Sodbury, turn left to take the A432 Chipping Sodbury road. Continue for a mile to reach the village centre. For parking, turn left immediately after the Dog Inn and opposite to the village green
Refreshments The Dog Inn, Old Sodbury; plus, several seats during the first half of the walk with panoramic views, suitable for picnics in the right weather conditions

---

A SCENIC RAMBLE along footpaths, through fields and by the riverside; and on quiet lanes through attractive villages. There is plenty of archaeological and historic interest, including Iron Age hill forts, manor houses and churches. Generally easy walking, with a couple of steep ascents of the Cotswolds ridge, that afford fine views over the surrounding countryside. There are a few muddy stretches towards the end of the walk.

The walk starts in the centre of the village of Old Sodbury. It proceeds north up the Cotswold Way towards the elevated church – from which there are extensive views towards the Severn Estuary – and continues along the escarpment to climb up to Soppa's Hill Fort (Sodbury Camp), one of the largest Iron Age hill forts in England. From here the route descends past Little Sodbury Manor and through the village towards Horton; from which you climb again to Horton Camp, a further Iron Age fort. You descend to reach Horton Court, a National Trust property with Norman origins. The route subsequently crosses numerous fields and farm complexes, picking up the Monarch's Way, to reach the fringes of Sodbury Common and Chipping Sodbury. The final stretch back to Old Sodbury is along the pleasant Frome Valley Walkway.

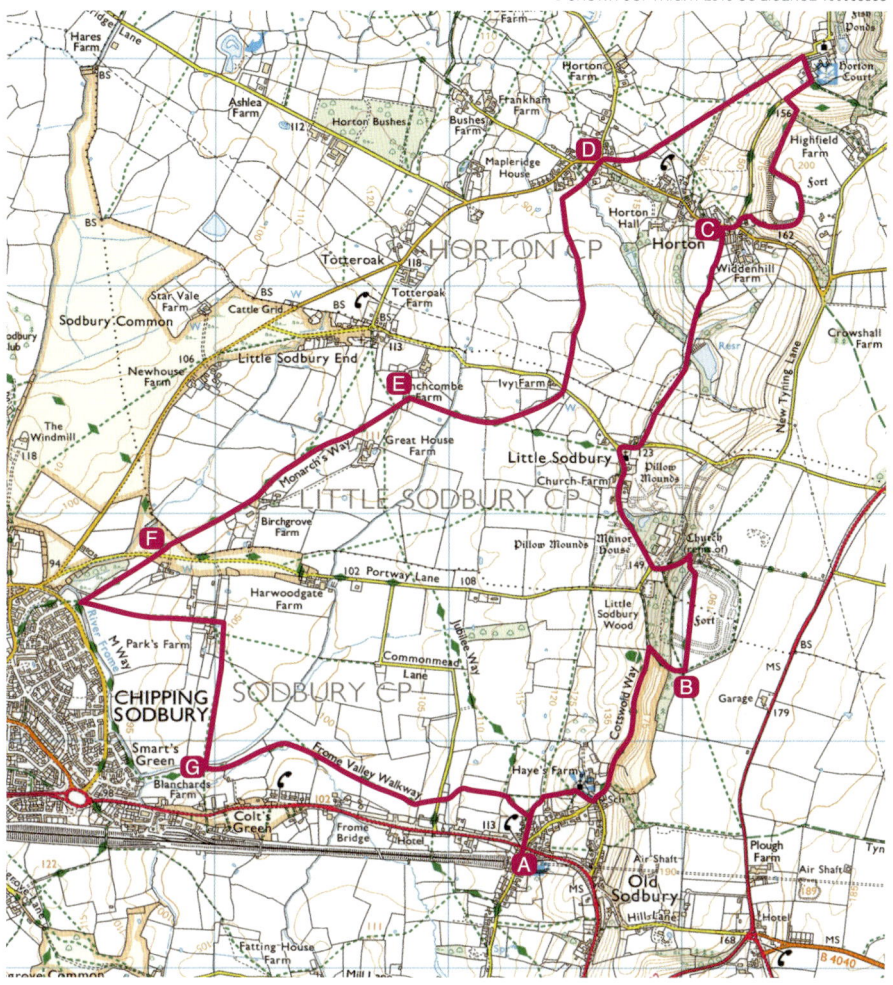

A From the Dog Inn cross the B4040 to the Green and Cotswold Lane. Follow the directions on the Cotswold Way footpath sign, to bear left down the walled driveway towards Church Farm. Pass The Mallards – various signs betray its associations with the former railway. Take the gate and go through the farmyard. Exit via the gate in the far right-hand corner into the field. Bear right and uphill, to take the small gate in the right-hand corner. In the next field, turn sharp right and up the steep grassy slope – towards the elevated St John the Baptist church. There are panoramic views towards Chipping Sodbury and the Severn Estuary. Take the gate ahead and walk through the churchyard, exiting via the main gate. Go down the lane, for about 30 metres. Turn left up the walled/fenced path, alongside the primary school. Pass through the fenced section, via gates at either end. Continue across the field in the same direction, for about 50 metres, and through the gate in the hedgerow. Enter the long field and proceed all the way along its top edge, with further

9

panoramic views. At the far corner, go through the gate to join the crossing path. Turn sharp right, following the Cotswold Way signs uphill into woodland. You now have a short, steep climb. At the top of the hill the path curves left to reach Soppa's Hill Fort, dating from about 500BC and subsequently strengthened by the Romans.

B Take the gate immediately ahead into the fort perimeter. The route takes you straight across the fort. You pass through gaps in the earthworks, towards the buildings of Woodcock Farm ahead. At the far perimeter turn left at the T-junction of paths, and exit, via the gate, into woodland. Follow the path, as it bends right and gradually descends alongside the farm buildings. Take the sharp left turn to descend more steeply into the woodland. Past the barn over to your right, initially keep with the main path as it forks to the left. However, just as the path starts curving back uphill, take the gate in the fence straight ahead. Keep downhill through the small orchard,

exiting, via the gate, on to the road below. Turn right along the road. (The driveway immediately off to the right leads to Little Sodbury Manor where William Tyndale, who translated the Bible into English in the early 1500s, once stayed.) Continue on down the wooded road. You soon pass through Little Sodbury village, including the church of St. Adeline. Beyond the church at the triangular road junction, turn right and uphill for about 100 metres. At the furthest of the terrace of cottages, turn left and go through to the rear of the garden. Exit via the stile into the field, in which you follow alongside the left-hand boundary. Continue through the gate into the next field. Keep ahead in the same direction and under the line of pylons. Take the gate in the left-hand corner and proceed into the following field. Pass the pond over to your right and continue downhill to cross the bridge. Keep left and go steeply up the slope. At the top, take the gate/stile to join the broad fenced track. Proceed in the direction of Horton

village, soon obvious ahead. When you reach the edge of the village, take the gate/stile to join the narrow, hedged track, leading on to the driveway and then out on to the main village street.

C Cross and turn right along the street, for about 50 metres. Take the uphill road off to the left and then the short cul-de-sac, up to the right. Go through the gate adjacent to the primary school, and up the fenced path with steps. At the top, take the gate into the field. Initially, keep along the right-hand boundary adjacent to the woodland. Stay with the path as it curves left and more steeply up the field, towards the tower – a folly. Continue uphill for about a further 50 metres, alongside the top left-hand boundary. Take the gate into the perimeter of Horton Camp, another Iron Age fort. Bear diagonally across the field, to the left-hand corner of the earthworks. At this corner turn right, as waymarked, to follow alongside the fence delineating the fort perimeter. Pass the bench and exit via the gate in the far corner, leading into woodland. Zig-zag steeply down the embankment and exit into the field below, via the gate. Turn sharp left and descend to take the stile next to the field gate. Exit on to the road, where you turn right and downhill. Follow the road as it bends left in front of Horton Court. This National Trust property has been extensively refurbished recently and is well worth a visit – however, opening is limited and you must book in advance. As the road bends around towards the main entrance and the adjacent church, turn sharp left, to take the footpath through the hedgerow and the gate. Go across the field, through the gap and up another field. Take the gate into the following field and keep straight ahead down this to exit, via the gate, in the bottom hedgerow. As you enter the next field, there is a fork in the paths. You head across the field, aiming for the small gate just to the right of a powerline pole. Take the gate and traverse the next, short field. Exit via another gate, to enter the following paddock. Proceed with the fence on your right, through the field gate and along the driveway, to pass various properties including Horseshoe Farm. Exit on to the main road immediately opposite to Horton Social Club, at the western extent of Horton village.

D Turn right along the main road for about 50 metres. Take the signed footpath off to the left, through the premises of Jasmine House. Exit, via the gate next to the garage, and follow the fenced path adjacent to the ditch. Turn sharp right, keeping alongside the boarded fencing. After about a further 30 metres, turn left across the ditch and through the hedgerow, into the very extensive field. Turn right along the hedgerow boundary, which you now follow along, for about 400 metres. Near to the far corner, exit through the gate in the hedgerow, into the next field. Bear slightly right across this field, passing under a major power line and aiming about 75 metres to the left of Ivy Farm ahead. Take the gate through the hedgerow. Traverse the following field to take the stone stile in the far boundary, on to the road ahead. Cross and take the similar stile immediately opposite. Continue ahead in the same direction, keeping to the right-hand boundary of the next field. Take the stile/footbridge/stile in the far hedgerow. In the subsequent field, turn right and continue alongside the right-hand boundary. Take the further stile/footbridge/stile into the next field. Keep with the right-hand boundary and pass through an often-waterlogged area to take yet another stile/footbridge/stile. The field beyond can also be waterlogged. Follow the waymarked route as best you can, through the middle of the field and towards the small gate in the far hedgerow, with Winchcombe Farm ahead and over to your right.

E Take the gate to enter the next field. Bear sharp left across the corner to take the stile in the hedgerow, into the adjacent field. With Great House Farm ahead, go diagonally towards the far right-hand corner, to take the stile hidden in the trees. Go through the orchard, cross the footbridge and the stile. Keep alongside the left-hand boundary of the following field, for about 200 metres in all. Near to the top left-hand corner, take the gate/footbridge/gate through the hedgerow. In the next field, keep alongside the right-hand boundary to take the gate adjacent to the farm outbuildings. Continue ahead through the farm complex and exit via the gate into the field beyond. Follow all along the left-hand boundary, with glimpses of Chipping Sodbury increasingly evident in the distance, to take the gate at the far end.

F Proceed straight-ahead across the open land. Go over the road and continue towards the gate in the far hedgerow. Take the gate and continue along the fenced path. At the end, take the gate/footbridge/gate into the meadow. Bear sharp left towards the boundary fence. Ignoring the field gate, proceed further along the boundary fence; to take the gap into the adjacent field. Proceed up the long left-hand field boundary, as waymarked. Follow through the gateway into the smaller field ahead. With farm buildings immediately to your left, go through the field gate. Head straight-across the paddock. Exit via the small gate by a tall hedge on to the driveway. Briefly turn right towards the entrance gate of Park Farm. Immediately, follow left around the outer edge of the grounds, as waymarked. Exit via the small gate into the open field ahead. Immediately, turn right and follow the track along the boundary; to take the gap into the next field. Turn right and closely follow the right-hand boundary through much of this extensive field. After skirting along woodland through

three field corners, follow the track by a long stretch of hedgerow – continuing all the way down the field to the obvious gap in the bottom boundary.

🅖 Pass through the gap in the hedgerow and over the bridge. Turn left, to join the crossing Frome Valley Walkway. Proceed along through the field, to take the gate/footbridge/gate in the hedgerow ahead. Continue along the next field, to take the gate/footbridge in the far hedgerow. With the river alongside, enter the large field and immediately turn right. After about 300 metres or so the path begins to take you away from the riverbank. Strike out across the field, to take the footbridge/gate in the far hedgerow. Cross the next field to take the gate/footbridge/gate. Pass through the small field to exit, via the gate, on to the crossing lane ahead. Cross and continue through the gate immediately opposite. Continue along the fenced footpath and exit, via the gate, into the field. With Old Sodbury church tower ever more evident, bear diagonally left across this field, to pick up the gate in the opposite hedgerow. Enter the next field and keep straight across it in the direction of the church. Take the gate into the corner of the following field, which you will recognise from earlier. Head diagonally towards the farm complex – following the line of posts and aiming to the left of the green farm building. Take the gate to revisit the farmyard and retrace your steps through it. As you exit, the Dog Inn is clearly visible along the driveway ahead. Re-cross the green and the main road to return to Chapel Lane, from where you started the walk. 🅐

No. 2

Stone, Ham and Whitcliff Park

Distance 6 miles / 9.5 kms
Time 2.5 to 3 hours
OS Map Explorer 167
Starting Point Stone village green – OS reference 684954
Parking Free parking on or near to village green
Reaching the start from Bristol Go north on the M5. Leave by Junction 14 and then go north along the A38 for a mile to the centre of the village of Stone. Turn left immediately before the church to reach the village green
Refreshments Salutation Inn, Ham

AN EASY RAMBLE alongside a peaceful river to the historic Berkeley Castle, thence through a medieval deer park, and back across fields to Stone. There is one short, gentle climb, affording panoramic views towards the Severn Estuary and the Cotswolds. In the first couple of fields the grass can be wet and tricky to traverse. Beyond here, though, the paths are all well-trodden albeit occasionally muddy.

The walk starts from Stone village green, from where you progress through the churchyard and out of the village – towards the Little Avon River. You follow alongside the river all the way to the edge of the town of Berkeley, enjoying attractive views of the castle as you approach. The walk then deviates southwards through the village of Ham, before climbing an escarpment and traversing the full length of the elevated Whitcliff Park. You descend out of the park, to traverse low-lying fields bounded by streams or ditches, and return in the direction of Stone via a series of stiles, fences and footbridges.

A From Stone village green, go through the gate into the churchyard of All Saints Church. Continue on the footpath to the far end of the church. Take the left-hand fork and zig-zag along the surfaced footpath to reach Stone Primary School. Carry on down the cul-de-sac, to the T-junction at the end. Turn left along the lane for nearly 300 metres. Turn right through a gate in the hedgerow to enter a very long field. Initially, follow the wooded right-hand boundary for about 150 metres. As the boundary becomes less wooded and curves away to the right, strike out diagonally along the field towards the gateway in the far left-hand corner. There is no clearly-defined route – make your way as best you can. Take the gateway into the next field. Continue with the hedge on your left for about 50 metres. At the hedge corner keep straight ahead in the same direction – down the centre of the open field – aiming for a group of trees by the river.

B At the field bottom turn left and walk along beside the Little Avon River, which you will now follow for the next 2500 metres or so. Go over the low fence into the next field and continue to Matford Bridge. Cross the bridge, go through the gate and now proceed with the Little Avon on your left. As you enter the next field, via the gate, Berkeley Castle is prominent in the distance. Proceed across a total of six fields via a series of gates, fences and stiles, keeping alongside the riverbank throughout. Tanhouse Farm appears over on the far bank and, a little beyond, Brownsmill Farm, which lies closer to the river. At around this point, a drainage ditch comes in from the right. Continue alongside the riverbank and in the same direction. Take successive field gates to reach the crossing track, extending across the bridge to Brownsmill Farm. Keep straight ahead, to take the stile/gate ahead into the following field. It can be very muddy at this point. Keep ahead along the right-

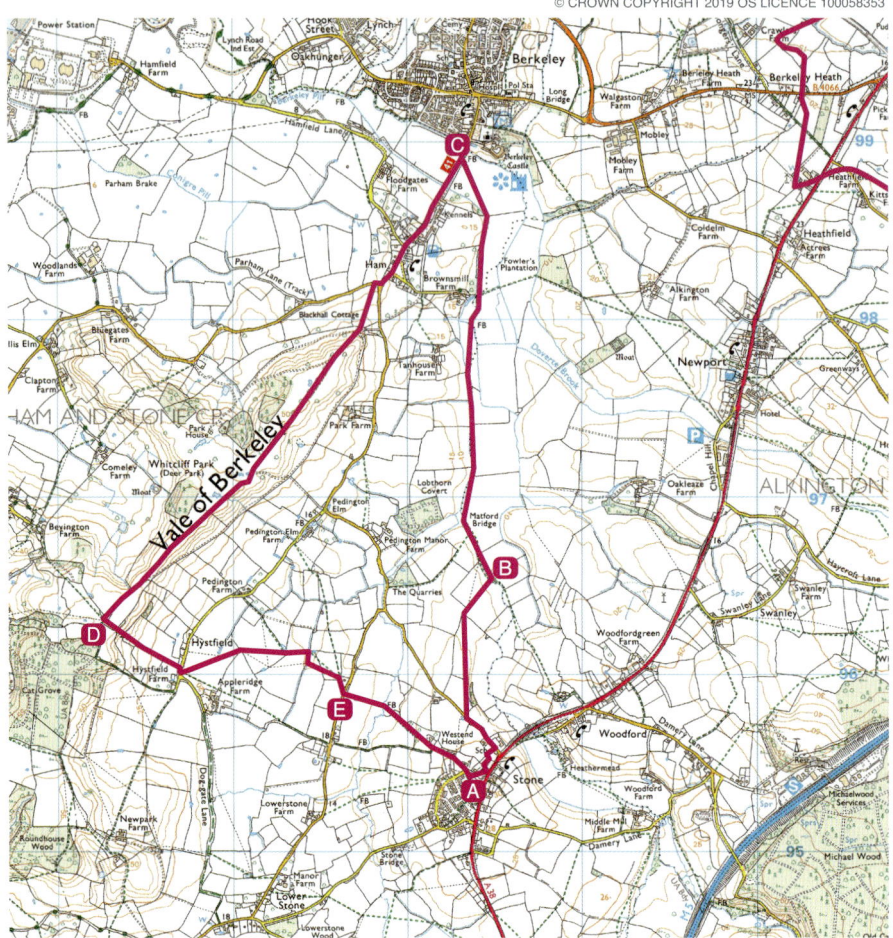

hand riverbank. With the castle becoming ever nearer, take the gate into the next field, immediately passing the concrete farm bridge off to your left. Now leave the riverbank and strike out diagonally towards the right-hand corner, keeping the castle to your right. The castle has been the historic seat of the Berkeley family since the 11th century. King Edward II was imprisoned and eventually murdered here in 1327. (If you have the time to spare, a visit is certainly worthwhile.) Aim for the metal gate in the far boundary and climb the built-in stile. Cross the bridge to reach the road ahead.

C Cross the road and turn left to follow the footway alongside. As the road goes over the Little Avon River the footway switches to the left-hand side. Proceed past the 18th-century stables and kennels of the Berkeley Hunt, to reach the hamlet of Ham. You pass (or rest at) the Salutation Inn and continue along the edge of the village green. About 100 metres further along, look out for the road junction off to the right, signposted to Clapton, Bevington and Hill. Take the adjacent gate/stile to enter the field. Head left past the pond and steeply uphill towards the walled park. Cross the

boundary wall by way of the wooden steps and gate, to enter Whitcliff Park, which was first enclosed as a private hunting/deer park towards the end of the 13th century. Follow the path and then the track uphill. The way forward is very clearly signed by means of a series of closely-spaced white posts. As you climb and the track levels out, there are views west to the River Severn and east to Nibley Knoll and the Tyndale Monument. Continue through the park in this general direction, for more than 2000 metres in all. Initially, keep along the line of chestnut trees. Continue in the same direction when the line peters out. The path gradually veers towards the edge of the escarpment. Continue, through the deer fence, and aim for a stand of evergreen holm oaks ahead. Beyond here, proceed alongside the further deer fence. As a grassy ride bears off to the right, keep ahead on the more obvious path, aiming just to the left of the house to reach the boundary wall ahead.

D Climb the steps and stile to exit the park. Immediately climb another stile, off to the left into scrubland. Follow the narrow path adjacent to the boundary wall. After about 75 metres, climb another stile. Continue alongside the wall until you reach the corner of the park boundary. Continue around the boundary wall for a couple of metres then bear downhill, following the right-hand kink in the path. Proceed downhill to exit the scrubland into the field ahead. Bear right and continue downhill towards the hedgerow ahead. Immediately look out for the convoluted stile/footbridge/stile, which you cross over to enter the adjacent field. Walk all the way down this long, sloping field with the hedgerow on your right. Take the double stile to access the road ahead. Cross towards the footpath sign diagonally opposite. Enter the following field, by way of the stile/footbridge/stile. Head half-left, aiming just to the right of an electricity pole and then a clump of trees and bushes. Continue in

the same direction to cross the stile/footbridge/stile in the far hedgerow. In the next field walk half-right to the far corner, keeping just to the right of an electricity pole. Cross the combination of stiles and footbridge. In the next field go straight ahead to follow the hedgerow on your left. Keep ahead, to take the substantial footbridge into the field beyond. Pass the pond and follow the left-hand field boundary as it bears around to the right. After about 100 metres take the further footbridge on the left into the following field. Bear towards the bungalow and the right-hand corner – with Stone church tower directly ahead in the distance. Turn right through the metal gate and into the following field. Proceed with the boundary on your left, towards another metal gate in the hedgerow. Cross the adjoining stile and footbridge to reach the road ahead.

E Cross the road and the bridge/stile combination opposite, into the next field. Walk down the field by the right-hand boundary. At the bottom keep ahead, to cross the stream, via the footbridge. Turn sharp right and cross the next field, to take the gate in the hedgerow. In the following field keep alongside the left-hand boundary. Take the stile in the left-hand corner to enter the curtilage of Westend House. Carry on through the former orchard, pass the house and pick up the surfaced driveway. Exit through the main gate. The drive morphs into a lane, which soon leads you back to your starting point, Stone village green. **A**

No. 3
Cheddar Gorge

Distance 7.5 miles / 12 kms
Time 4 to 4.5 hours
OS Map Explorer 141
Starting Point Cheddar Head – OS reference 494533
Parking Free parking at Cheddar Head lay-by on the B3135, just opposite the junction with the B3371
Reaching the start from Bristol Go south on the A38. Pass Bristol Airport. Just over half-a-mile beyond the Holiday Inn, take the minor road off to the left, signed to Burrington. Turn right at T-junction with the A368. Ignoring the first road off to the left, signed to Burrington village, take the second turn soon afterwards. Go up Burrington Combe on the B3134. Continue until you reach the right-hand B3371 turn, signed to Cheddar. Continue along the B3371 for about two miles, to reach the T-junction with the B3135 at Cheddar Head. Turn right and immediately enter the lay-by
Refreshments Riverside Inn, Cheddar; with other options in Cheddar

---

THIS IS A CHALLENGING CIRCULAR WALK with some steep climbs. The walk passes via three diverse nature reserves and includes spectacular views down into Cheddar Gorge, over towards the Somerset Levels and well beyond. There is an often-muddy stretch along the Gorge, between Cheddar and Black Rock Gate.

The walk starts at Cheddar Head, from which you climb up an old Mendip drove, to the southern edge of the Mendips with views over the Levels and way beyond. You join the West Mendip Way and slowly descend along it to Cheddar village and the foot of the gorge. There follows a prolonged climb up to the northern edge of the gorge. You continue along this edge of the gorge, to cross at Black Rock Gate. You climb steeply again up the other side and then descend again, via Bubwith Nature Reserve. The final section undulates along the Gorge, via the Middledown Nature Reserve, broadly parallel with the B3135 and back to Cheddar Head.

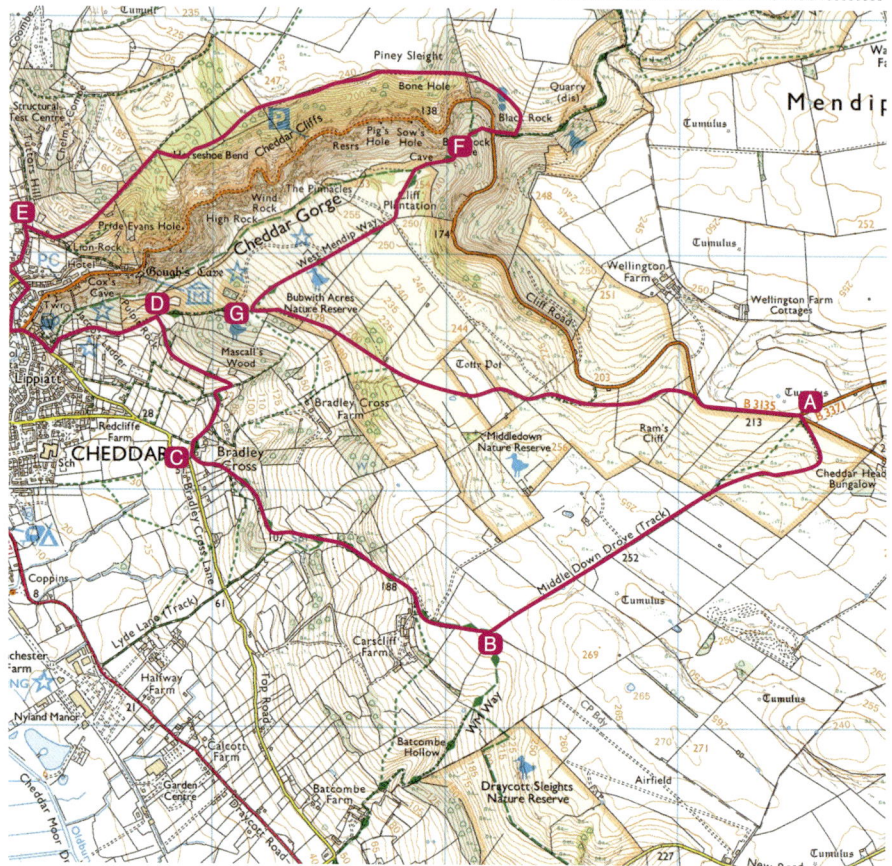

A From the lay-by go back towards the road junction and take the gate opposite. Bear left up the hillside on the more obvious track, Middle Down Drove. Climb gently up the broad track as it meanders left and right. As you near the top of the hillside, pass the substantial dew pond on your right. Proceed through the gate and along the now walled track/green lane. You soon pass Middledown Nature Reserve off to your right. As you continue ahead sweeping views unfold across to Nyland Hill, the Somerset Levels, the Polden Hills, Brent Knoll, Crook Peak and Wales. Near the edge of the escarpment you arrive at a T-junction in front of a field gate – at which the West Mendip Way cuts in from the east – to join the track.

B Turn right and continue downhill on the track, towards Cheddar and Cheddar Reservoir. Take the gate into the open field and continue steeply downhill, passing farm buildings on the left. Cross a muddy track and take the metal gate straight ahead. Advance down the sunken track through woodland. Upon reaching a pond take the gate into the field ahead. Proceed towards the fence/hedge which you now follow down the field alongside – on the grassy track. The track eventually bends around to the right, adjacent to woodland, and drops further towards the field gate. Follow through into the next field and continue downhill until the field narrows towards another gate at the bottom. Go through on to the hedged track, leading down to the junction of tracks at Bradley Cross.

C Turn right immediately in front of Bradley Cottage. Continue along the track which begins to climb. Follow the West Mendip Way signs in the Cheddar direction. After passing Bradley Hill House on your right, bear left at the fork. Carry on, through the gate and past Owley, to reach the T-junction by some sheds. Turn right up the grassy path. After about 50 metres turn left, to take the path into Mascall Woods. Follow the fenced path around the hillside, for about 400 metres in all, passing in and out of woodland/scrubland. Just before a gate you pass the remains of a lime kiln. Go through the gate and soon take another one, to join a wide, hedged lane running down the hillside.

D Turn left down the green lane. Continue through the gate ahead. As you reach the edge of the village of Cheddar the track merges into a metalled driveway, coming down the hill from the right. At the waymark post keep left and downhill. Within about 50 metres, at Copse Cottage take the right-hand turn down the ginnel – which drops down, eventually by steps, on to another lane. Turn right down the walled lane to the centre of the village. At the T-junction turn left and across the bridge. (If you wish to stop at the Riverside Inn, this is immediately over to the left). Resuming on the route from the far side of the bridge, take the first right-hand turn immediately beyond the fish and chip shop. Continue uphill to soon enjoy good views of the village and across the Cheddar Gorge. Beyond the seat off to the right, keep left around

the bend in the lane and past the row of cottages. Just beyond the cottages turn right up Tuttors Hill. Climb for just over 150 metres, bending left and right as the road steepens, to reach the entrance to Rockland House on your left.

E Turn right, to take the surfaced driveway oppposite. After about 100 metres, at Cufic House the drive diverges into two paths. Fork left with the upper path. Go through the gate and into the woodland. You now embark on a sustained ascent, keeping towards the right-hand boundary wall until eventually taking the obvious gate through it. Proceed on the level for about 100 metres and then bear sharply left, up a lesser path. Continue alongside the same boundary wall, but with it now on your left. Keep on the soon obvious path uphill towards the top of the gorge. Take the stile at the corner junction of the wall and, immediately, the hairpin bend through the gateway into the open area adjacent to the gorge. Follow along the right-hand wall for about 50 metres. At this point, pick up the track emerging from the field gate on your right. Bear left, to follow the track uphill and towards the far boundary wall. Stay on this track as it continues uphill, alongside/parallel with the wall. There are superb views over into the gorge, which is the largest in Britain and its cliffs the highest inland cliffs. Pass the waymark post. Continue on uphill, keeping towards scrubland and the gorge, on your right. At the top of this prolonged climb take the small gate in the wall ahead. Continue straight ahead along the path, with the fence on your left and the open semi-wooded slopes of the gorge down to your right. Eventually the path takes you on a steep descent, including down a long flight of steps. At the bottom of the steps go straight ahead, to take the gate in the wall and proceed through the

small copse. Keep ahead on the path, passing through motley open land, scrub and woodland. Take the gate ahead to enter the woodland of the Black Rock Nature Reserve, home to a wide variety of wild flowers and trees. You eventually drop down steeply through a gate to the junction with the crossing track below. Turn right to join the broad stony track and immediately take the field gate. Within about 100 metres exit via the further gate to reach Black Rock Gate.

F Cross straight over the road. Bear slightly right towards the obvious rocky track opposite. Climb the track steeply up through woodland. Stick with the main track as it curves around to the left and continues uphill. Pass the outcrop of rock over to your left. Take the gate just beyond, to exit into further open land. Initially continue adjacent to the woodland. After about 50 metres, take the left-hand fork signed towards Draycott. Continue gently uphill on this grassy path, through the open land for about a further 250 metres. Continue over a crossing track and uphill, to take the stile hidden in the left-hand corner. In the next field bear slightly right, to pick up the broad, grassy path ahead. This leads you down through gorse bushes with spectacular panoramic views over the Somerset Levels. Go through the gate ahead to enter Bubwith Acres Nature Reserve. Drop downhill on the same green track, all the way down to reach another information board at the bottom, just before the exit gate.

G From the information board, turn sharp left back upon yourself to re-climb the hillside. Follow the indistinct path as it initially skirts the gorse and bracken over to the right. After no more than 75 metres continue ahead to follow the less obvious fork into the undergrowth. This path can become overgrown but with persistence should always prove passable. It soon emerges to join a grassy track. Keep ahead on the track and through the field gate, and continue for about a

further 400 metres. Contour the edge of the hill, before climbing through the bracken and trees, to take the stile in the left-hand fence by the further information board. Exit the reserve and bear right, up the rough open field. There are rocks and another old lime kiln over to your right. Keep across to the far wall and through the field gate. Bear leftwards across the next field, passing the lone ash tree on your left and the shed and the pond on your right. Take the gate through the hedgerow ahead. Cross the next field in the same direction. You are now within the Middledown Nature Reserve, which you skirted earlier. Take successive gates to enter the overgrown area, which incorporates Totty Pot, a Mesolithic burial site. Turn right to follow the inner edge of the monument perimeter. Exit via the gate/barrier leading out to the right. Bear left down the field on an indistinct path, to join the obvious track crossing below. Follow the track downhill, keeping broadly parallel with the main road, now clearly evident over to your left. When the track bends sharply left and further downhill, keep straight ahead, to leave it. Continue on the path, uphill and along the hillside – in parallel with the main road. Take the gate in the boundary wall. Keep on the path through bracken and scrub, still parallel with the road below. Cross the following boundary wall into the next field. Bear diagonally left down the field to the obvious stile in the far corner. Cross the stile, to reach the road. Turn right alongside the B3135 for about 250 metres, to return to the Cheddar Head lay-by. **A**

No. 4

Tintern and Brockweir

Distance 6.75 miles / 10.5 kms
Time 3.5 hours
OS Map Explorer OL14
Starting Point Tintern Abbey, Tintern – OS reference 533002
Parking Tintern Abbey all-day car park. Parking charges apply. The charge is refundable if money is spent in the Abbey or the Anchor Inn
Reaching the start from Bristol Go west on the M4. Exit by Junction 21, to take the M48 over the River Severn. Exit by Junction 2, then continue on the A466 northwards, passing Chepstow racecourse. On reaching Tintern, follow the car park signs on the right, to the abbey
Refreshments The Old Station, between Brockweir and Tintern; or various options in Tintern, including the Anchor Inn, Abbey Mill, the Rose and Crown or the Royal George Hotel

---

THIS WALK, CENTRED ON THE DRAMATIC RUINS OF TINTERN ABBEY, gives you a taste of the beauty of the Wye Valley. The route follows woodland tracks and paths, plus an open riverside stretch. There is one prolonged steep ascent, but this proves rewarding.

The walk starts next to the abbey, from which you soon cross the river into woodland on the other side. You proceed by the river along the route of a disused tramway – before climbing steeply to pick up the Offa's Dyke path, from which there are spectacular views down to both the abbey and the river. You gradually descend back towards Brockweir – where you cross back over the river. The walk concludes directly alongside the river, as you pass through meadows and much of Tintern, before returning to the abbey.

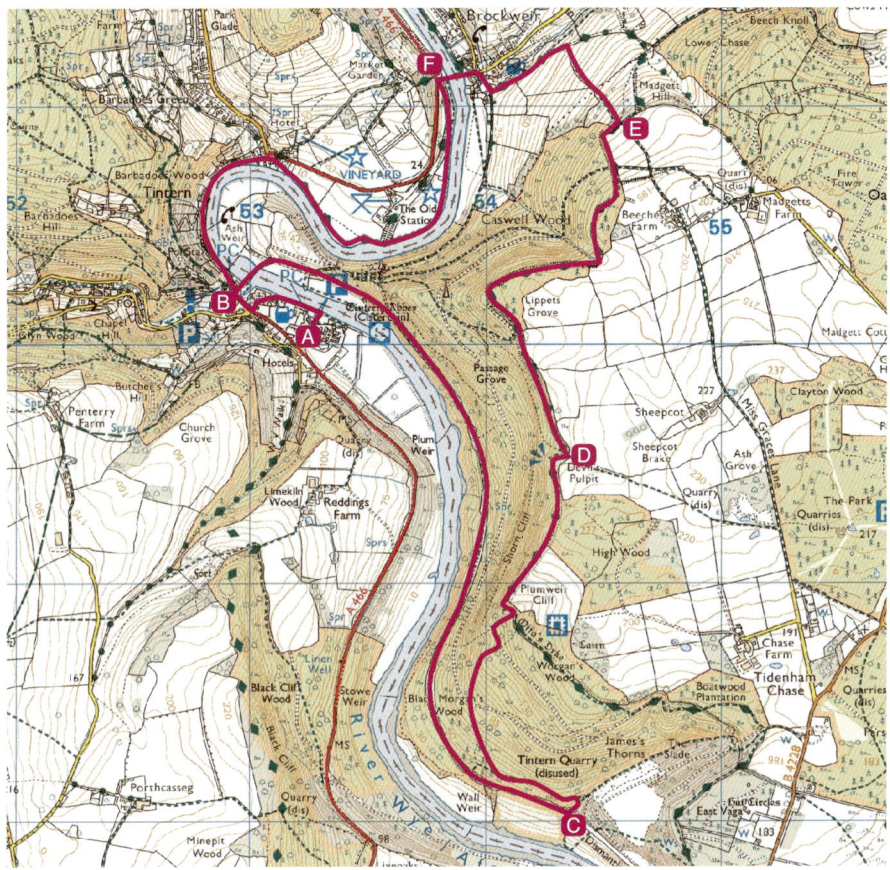

A From Tintern Abbey car park, take the riverside path between the Anchor Inn and the River Wye. You soon divert away from the river along the lane between cottages, at the end of which you turn left and uphill, to reach the A466. Turn right along the main road, past the doctors' surgery and Abbey Mill.

B Immediately beyond the Abbey Mill access road, turn right on the track leading back towards the river. Cross the broad bridge ahead. This originally carried the tramway from the former ironworks nearby – Tintern was not always the rural idyll one might imagine! After the bridge crossing, the track bends right and enters woodland. Follow the disused tramway/railway track alongside the riverbank, for about 3000 metres in all, ignoring all paths off to the left and right. There are scenic glimpses through the woodland of the abbey on the other side of the river. The tunnel over to the left signals the emergence of the track of the former Wye Valley Railway. Much further beyond, you continue across the wire-fenced bridge. From here, the track gradually descends via the cutting ahead to an obvious junction.

C At the junction bear left, to take the uphill track and leave the disused railway. At the next junction, after about 150

25

metres, keep sharp left along the same track. Continue uphill for about a further 250 metres, to reach the multi-junction from which the way forward is not immediately obvious. Take the lesser path straight ahead through the undergrowth. Climb up through woodland on the mostly well-defined path. The broad direction is clear, but the precise route needs careful attention. A couple of minor deviations from the original route are necessary in order to accommodate changes in the undergrowth. The path bends gradually rightwards as it progresses inexorably up the hillside. You eventually reach a T-junction with a crossing path. Go left and down this broad path for just over 100 metres. As the main path bends sharply left, take the path leading up to the right. Climb with the aid of the rough steps and zig-zag further up the hillside. Keep climbing, as glimpses of the river arise ahead and over to your left. Continue uphill until you arrive at the Offa's Dyke. The path does continue leftwards along the original Offa's Dyke. However, there is also a broad stony track ahead that runs alongside it, which is easier to traverse. Offa's Dyke was built by Offa, King of Mercia between 757 and 796 AD. It formed a rough boundary between the Anglian kingdom of Mercia and the Welsh kingdom of Powys – and stretched 182 miles. If you prefer, you can proceed for some distance along the original path, more or less on top of the dyke. Eventually, however, you will be forced to switch to the parallel, newer, surfaced track. Whichever route you follow, continue to climb uphill slowly alongside the gorge. The track passes through a gateway in a wall, just beyond which a path joins in from the right. Beyond here the track levels out and begins to descend. As another track joins from the right, you should begin to have good views of Tintern Abbey, far below. You soon reach the Devil's Pulpit.

D The Devil's Pulpit, a rocky pinnacle, offers the clearest view of the abbey. Legend goes that the Devil taunted the monks at Tintern Abbey from here. Continue on down the path as it curves right, to reach the metal gate at the path junction. Proceed left down the steps and across the footbridge. Keep ahead through the woodland alongside the valley. Descend to the waymarked junction, from which a path branches off back down to Tintern (do not take this). Advance straight ahead on the Offa's Dyke path – leading to Brockweir and St. Briavels. Continue through similar terrain. Pass Lippets Grove Nature Reserve on your right. Further along, you come immediately alongside the edge of an open field. The path veers leftwards from this boundary. Continue along the top of the hillside on the, raised again, Offa's Dyke. Descend to reach the crossing path (from which Beeches Camp Site is signed off to the right). Keep straight ahead and downhill, towards the field corner beyond. Follow the field boundary around to the right. Within about 50 metres climb the stile. Continue alongside the field boundary for about 50 metres. On reaching the crossing path, marked by the stile in the field boundary, turn left and downhill. Take the gate at the bottom to finally exit the woodland into the following field.

E From the top of the field, you can see Brockweir and its bridge down to your left – with a whitewashed house standing alone to the right of the village. Bear diagonally left down the field towards the house, climbing the stile in the fence in the bottom left-hand corner. Continue down the following field – keeping towards the hedge on the left and taking the field gate ahead. Turn left on to the broad crossing track. Continue on downhill and through the gateway. Pass

agricultural outbuildings to reach the T-junction with the lane ahead. Turn right and follow the lane into the centre of the village of Brockweir, reaching the Brockweir Inn on your left. After passing the inn, keep left towards the road bridge to cross the river.

F On the far side, before reaching the main A466, descend the concrete steps on the left. At the bottom ignore the route of the disused Wye Valley Railway straight ahead. Follow the left-hand sign to 'Tintern via the riverbank'. Take the gate into the meadow. Proceed along the riverbank with the river on your left. Keep ahead, through the gate and into the following meadow. Over to the right you can see the restored former signal box within the former Wye Valley Railway station, which has been converted to a café and museum. (If you wish to detour here, simply turn right in the direction of the obvious buildings, as soon as you enter the field. Otherwise carry on through the meadow, continuing along the walkway by the river.) Go

through the gate, pass the remains of the demolished railway bridge and take another gate. For a brief stretch the path is paved. Beyond here, the path can become muddy after heavy rain or if the river has been in flood. Continue ahead, crossing over several interspersed footbridges in the general direction of Tintern Parva. Take the gate to enter the churchyard of St. Michael's Church. Continue through the churchyard and exit on to the lane. Past Parva farmhouse, immediately fork left to pass between cottages and reach the A466 again. Most of the remainder of the walk runs alongside the main road. Turn left and keep ahead on the pavement. You pass some interesting buildings and shops, with the river always in sight. Narrow or non-existent footways at some points, necessitate your proceeding with care and selectively criss-crossing the road. After passing (or stopping at) the Rose and Crown, you soon find yourself back at Abbey Mill. Just beyond here, you re-take the lane down past the doctors' surgery. Bear right along the waymarked fork, back towards the river. Retrace your steps along the riverbank. Return to the car park and the abbey. **A**

Before you depart, it is well worth visiting Tintern Abbey. The abbey was founded in 1131 and operated until the dissolution of the monasteries in 1536.

No. 5
Aust, Littleton and Oldbury

Distance 10 miles / 16 kms
Time 4.5 hours
OS Map Explorer 167
Starting Point Outside the Boars Head, Main Road, Aust – OS reference 574890
Parking Free parking area; at the far eastern end of Main Road, Aust – or other opportunities elsewhere along Main Road
Reaching the start from Bristol Go west on the M4. Exit by Junction 21. Take the M48. Exit by Junction 1. Turn left on the A403. Almost immediately turn left again to enter Main Road, Aust
Refreshments Boars Head, Aust; or White Hart, Littleton; or the Anchor Inn, Oldbury; or seats with panoramic views at Cowhill church

---

A MOSTLY FLAT WALK, principally along country tracks and lanes, with one prolonged climb and a couple of shorter ones. Panoramic views throughout, most especially from the elevated churchyard at Cowhill. As well as this ideal picnic stop, there is a strong choice of pubs. Parts of the walk can be muddy.

The walk starts at Aust village. The initial section proceeds across farmland and via a green lane to the village of Littleton-upon-Severn. From here, the route bears up Sacks Hill and along Stock Hill – from which you head northwards, along another green lane, to the prominent Cowhill church. With Oldbury Power Station in the background, you descend into the village of Oldbury-upon-Severn and advance along Oldbury Pill to the Severn Estuary. The route follows along the estuary for a stretch of about 2.5 miles – eventually climbing up to the Severn Bridge. You skirt the Severn View Services, before returning to Aust village.

A Start from outside the Boars Head in Main Road, Aust – facing towards the church. Immediately take the adjacent road off to the right, Sandy Lane. Proceed past various houses. After about 150 metres turn right. Continue via the underpass under the M48, to reach the B4461 slip road. Cross the road, go through another underpass and over the cattle grid. Take the driveway ahead up to Manor Farm. Keep straight ahead through a mixture of offices and farm buildings. Exit at the far end, via the gate into the following field. Continue uphill, adjacent to the right-hand boundary. On reaching the field corner maintain the same direction across the open field to reach the far hedgerow. Turn sharp right along the boundary and down to the field gate in the corner. Take the gate and continue through the small field, now following the right-hand hedgerow. Exit over the gate to reach the crossing farm track. Turn left and continue through Cote Farm, via three field gates.

B Just beyond Cote Farm, turn right up the short track, to take the stile/gate into the field. Proceed along the right-hand hedge, to pick up the stile in the far corner. Go over and, in the next field, stick with the right-hand hedgerow, as the path bends left and right. Take the gate and cross the bridge over the rhyne. Advance along the hedged green lane. Stay on the lane, as it bends left and right (ignoring a fork, straight ahead through a field gate). Upon reaching the built-up area of Littleton-upon-Severn, go through the field gate and soon join the main village street. Turn left and continue along the street for about 250 metres, to reach the White Hart pub.

C About 100 metres beyond the pub, turn right along the drive/lane. Pass Willow Barn and ignore the first stile off to the left, immediately beyond. About 50 metres further along take the path off to the left, through the hedge and the gate, into the adjacent field. Keep to the right-hand hedge and continue through another gate to enter the next field, with the escarpment up ahead. Bear right across the field, aiming just to the left of the central power pole. Exit via the stile onto the lane, which you cross, to take the stile opposite and enter the large field opposite. Proceed up the escarpment – keeping with the right-hand boundary and climbing steeply up to the top. Go through the scrub to the corner to take the stile into the copse. Immediately turn left at the junction of paths. Take the gate into the following, extensive field. Turn right and follow the field boundary, for about 150 metres. About halfway down the field, just beyond the leftwards kink in the boundary edge, take the field gate into the adjacent woodland, to join the crossing path/track. Turn left and continue downhill. The path descends gradually, before emerging from the woodland, via the gate, into the field ahead. Continue straight ahead, up the track. At the top, go through two more gates and continue on the same track through the next field. At the far boundary, take the gate immediately off to the left. Go through the hedge and a second gate to reach the following field. Cross diagonally to take the gate near to the far corner and meet the crossing ancient track, Bond Lane.

D Turn left on this green lane and keep along it for about 700 metres in all. As you advance along the ridge, there are extensive views of the Cotswolds over to the right. Follow the lane, as it descends through a cutting and a copse. Pass Avening Cottage to soon reach the road ahead. Turn left and continue uphill, for about 300 metres. As the road bends sharply to

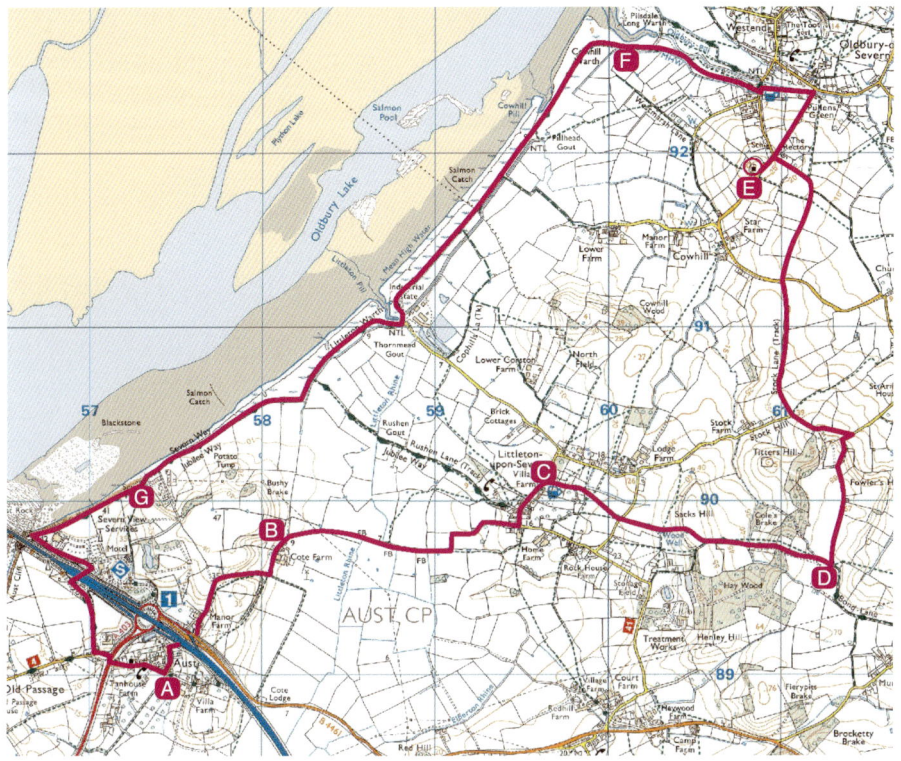

the left, with views opening up of the estuary ahead, go straight ahead down the green lane, Stock Lane. Cowhill church, towards which you will now be heading, soon appears on the horizon – with Oldbury Power Station in the background. Keep ahead down the lane, as it broadens out. The ground can be very uneven in places. Go through the gate, cross the road and continue through the blockade of rocks. Keep on the green lane for at least a further 500 metres, until reaching a T-junction with a crossing track. Turn left and proceed uphill, with St Alrida's church becoming increasingly prominent ahead. Upon reaching the road, cross on to the footway and proceed uphill towards the church.

E Take the gate into the churchyard, from which there are spectacular views over the surrounding countryside and across a large swathe of the Severn Estuary. Circle around the churchyard to experience its full setting. There are plenty of seats spread around, from which to enjoy the panorama. Eventually, take the steps down to and through the back gates. Turn left around the perimeter back towards the road. Turn left, along the road/footway, retracing your steps back down to the junction you emerged from earlier. This time continue straight ahead over the road to take the gate into the field ahead. Go down the field and through the gate in the far hedgerow. In the next field keep on down the right-hand field boundary. Exit via the gate in the far right-hand corner. Take the fenced path past stables.

Exit via the gate and cross the track, to reach Oldbury Pill. Turn left, to follow the hedged/fenced path along the pill edge. Continue ahead to take the gate into the extensive garden area. Exit through the gate at the far end. Pass through the petanque boules court and the garden/car park of the Anchor Inn. Turn left along the road, for about 50 metres. Take the right-hand turn through gates – and proceed along the surfaced track. Continue past the chalet. Pass through successive field gates. Keep ahead with the hedged/fenced track, past various further buildings and structures. Go through more gates (often left open), as Oldbury Pill reappears and gradually widens out, down to your right. Keep ahead, as the track becomes grassy. Eventually you emerge through a further gate into open land, next to Oldbury Pill.

F From the gate, initially, keep alongside the left-hand hedge – then, head straight towards the waymark post, on top of the embankment. Turn left along the embankment, with Cowhill Warth over to your right. Now simply follow along the Severn Estuary towards the Severn Bridge, for 4000 metres or so. Pass a well-signed turning off to the left and subsequently go through two sets of gates ahead. At Littleton Warth, the embankment bends inland, towards an industrial estate. Keep with the path, crossing the warth and passing through the gate. Continue on the embankment in the direction of the Severn Bridge. As you pass another exit off to the left, the main path meanders further away from the estuary. After the path/embankment bends back inwards, look out for the derelict railway wagon on the shoreline. From here, continue for at least a further 500 metres – until reaching a field gate ahead of the exposed river cliffs by the bridge.

G Turn left through the gate and proceed up the field, keeping to within about 30 metres of the right-hand hedgerow. Take the gate in the top right-hand corner. Keep going through another field next to the right-hand hedgerow. Exit via the gate and go through the copse to emerge in an overgrown area on the fringes of the original Severn View Services. You can see ahead of you what was originally the main building of the services, now converted to offices. Advance through the scrubland, to join the concrete path. Turn right and keep along the edge. You reach the viewing area, incorporating the plaque commemorating the opening of the bridge in 1966. Continue left around the bend. Carry on for about 300 metres, now walking parallel with the M48. As you approach the services' petrol station, turn right down the steps and across the pedestrian bridge over the M48. At the other side of the bridge, turn left. Keep on the tarmac path, parallel with the motorway, for about 100 metres. Pass through bollards, to reach the service/access road. Turn right and continue past the maintenance depot, to reach the highway. Turn left and proceed to the A403 at the bottom. With Aust village visible ahead, carefully cross the A403 via the traffic island. Proceed straight ahead to rejoin the main village street, from which you started the walk. Passing the village hall and the church on your left, simply carry on up Main Road, until you reach your vehicle. **A**

No. 6

Brent Knoll and Berrow Sands

Distance 11 miles / 18 kms

Time 5 to 5.5 hours

OS Map Explorer 153

Starting Point St Mary's Church, Church Road, East Brent – OS reference 344518.

Parking Free on-street parking along Church Road or along other roads nearby

Reaching the start from Bristol Go south on the M5. Exit by Junction 22. Turn right on the A38 for two miles. Bear left at the roundabout, to take the A370, signed to East Brent. After about half-a-mile, turn left at the traffic lights into the village. Proceed until you reach Church Road, leading towards the church, on the left

Refreshments Towards the end of the walk, a short detour can be made to the Red Cow, Brent Knoll village. Several good opportunities for picnics, especially along Berrow Sands

---

THIS DEMANDING BUT SPECTACULAR WALK is centred on Brent Knoll, which dominates the surrounding landscape and from which height you can see the rest of the route – across the western Somerset Levels to Burnham, along Berrow Beach and back across the Levels to East Brent – and far beyond. Whilst this walk should be easily traversible throughout most of the year, a short section across the Somerset Levels from Berrow can become muddy, especially after prolonged rainfall.

The walk starts in East Brent, from which you steeply ascend Brent Knoll. The subsequent descent to Brent Knoll village is similarly steep. From the village, you venture out on to the Somerset Levels. The route passes through numerous fields before tracking in the direction of the lighthouses and seaside at Burnham. There follows a lengthy section along Berrow Sands, with panoramic views across the Bristol Channel. You revert inland and back out on to the Levels. There follows a long, straight track/lane back towards the foot of Brent Knoll. You climb briefly again, before contouring the knoll through fields/scrubland, prior to the final descent through the churchyard and back into East Brent.

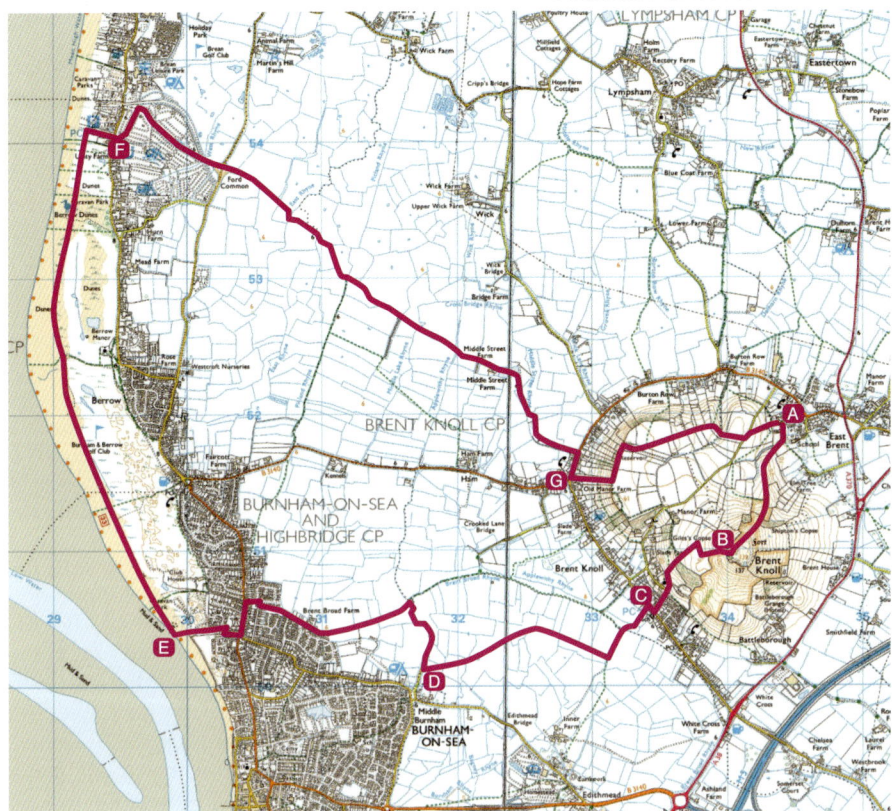

© CROWN COPYRIGHT 2019 OS LICENCE 100058353

A Go through the main gates of St Mary's Church into the churchyard. Immediately turn left, alongside the wall. Take the gate, to enter the fenced footpath, skirting around the primary school playground. Take another gate. Bear right with the fenced path as it bends alongside the pond/stream. Exit via the further gate into the adjacent field. Keep with the left-hand boundary, and take the stile to enter the much larger field. Bear slightly leftwards up the obvious path, to start the ascent of Brent Knoll. Go through the gate in the left-hand corner of the hedgerow. Climb more steeply in the next field, alongside the left-hand hedge. Take the following gate to enter National Trust open land. Continue steeply uphill in the same direction, aiming for the wooden pole on the top. Proceed clockwise around the summit of Brent Knoll, circumnavigating the ramparts of the Iron Age fort. The views can be spectacular. On a clear day you can see the Mendips, across the Somerset Levels to Glastonbury Tor, and towards the coast and over the Severn Estuary. You should have a clear overview of the route ahead, including the white, former Berrow lighthouse, a frequently re-occurring landmark during the first third of the walk. The topograph aids identification of the 360-degree view. Proceed to the Jubilee Bonfire stone. Beyond here, continue clockwise around the earthworks for about a further 75 metres. Watch out for the steps.

B Turn left and descend steeply via the steps. Exit the open land perimeter, via the gate. Follow the fenced path downwards, as it bends around the left edge of consecutive fields. Initially the descent remains steep – the path can be slippery in wet conditions. At the bottom of the second field keep straight ahead through the gate and continue downhill. At the bottom take the left-hand gate. Follow the fenced path down through trees and alongside the boundary wall of the churchyard, towards Brent Knoll village. Go through the gate next to St Michael's Church, to emerge on to Church Lane. Turn left and follow the road downhill to the main road ahead. Cross and turn right. Proceed for about 75 metres, to reach the footpath sign, just beyond the 30-mph speed limit sign.

C Turn left and take the short track. Go through the gate into the following field and keep alongside the right-hand boundary. Cross the stile/footbridge/stile, to emerge out in the open levels. Proceed along the fenced footpath. Go through the gate and, within about 50 metres, turn left over the stile/footbridge/stile, to cross the rhyne into the adjacent field. Proceed along the right-hand hedgerow until you reach the stile on the right, next to the field gate. Cross the stile, the track and the stile/gate opposite to enter a long field. Keep on the path ahead, alongside the hedgerow. Take the gate into the next field. Continue ahead, with the boundary on your right. On reaching the hedge corner, advance across the remainder of the field to take the bridge in the far hedgerow. In the field beyond bear sharp left to take the white gate, adjacent to the railway. Carefully cross the railway line. On the other side, take the gate ahead. Bear slightly left across the following field, to take the gate/footbridge/gate in the far boundary. Proceed in a similar direction across the next field. Take the further bridge through the hedge, into the subsequent field. Continue in the same direction, to take the gate/bridge in the far hedgerow. Exit on to the crossing track.

D Turn right and follow the winding hedge-lined track for about 600 metres. When you reach the T-junction, turn left and immediately go through the gate. This surfaced track follows the rhyne on the left all the way to the built-up area of Berrow/Burnham-on-Sea. Go through two field gates and keep ahead – past various houses and back gardens – as the track morphs into more of an access road. You eventually reach a T-junction with an estate road. Turn right, then almost immediately left, along Shelley Drive to reach Berrow Road, the main B3139. You soon see the former lighthouse over to the right. This pillar lighthouse has been inactive since 1993 and is now a private house. It lies 500 metres to the east of the low lighthouse, which has now replaced it – you will shortly be passing this also. Cross and turn left along Berrow Road for about 200 metres. Take the second turning on the right, Gore Road, marked 'no vehicular access to the beach'. Proceed on the right-hand footway to the end of the road. Keep with the footpath as it curves off to the right and winds behind the houses. You reach the beach with the second lighthouse straight ahead.

E Turn right, to continue the walk along the extensive Berrow Sands. Keep along the beach for almost 4000 metres. There are plenty of opportunities to stop and admire the views along the way. Bridgwater Bay and the Devon coast should be immediately apparent. In due course you should be able to see Steep Holm and Flat Holm, the two islands out in the Bristol Channel, and the high-rise buildings of Cardiff and the South Wales coast over on the opposite shore. The final part of the beach walk passes through the wooden/concrete posts that delineate the end of the Berrow Beach car park. Continue along the beach, all the way to the far end of the car park. Here, turn right to leave the coast via the beach access road. You pass the Beachside Holiday Park on the way to the main road. Cross, and continue right for about 50 metres to reach the main entrance of the Holiday Resort Unity Caravan Park.

F Follow the waymarked route along the entrance road into the park, passing the takeaway and entertainment complex. Continue on for about a further 150 metres – at which point follow the road as it turns sharply to the right alongside the stream. Cross the junction, beyond which the road morphs into a fenced walkway. Go past the fishing lake, through the gate and across the park road. Keep straight ahead, on the path between the rhyne and the copse. Cross the road and continue ahead on the surfaced track opposite. You are now back out on the open levels. Take the gate and keep along the elevated track between rhynes, with Brent Knoll ahead in the distance. After going through the next field gate, the surfaced track gradually morphs into a green lane, still between rhynes. This section of the walk can be muddy. Continue through the following gate, to reach successive field gates at a junction of paths and rhynes. Keep straight ahead, through the gates and across the rhyne. Continue on the green lane to go through the next field gate ahead. Henceforth, the track is more of a road, Middle Street, which you follow all the way along to the other end. Go over a further rhyne and continue past the recently planted John's Wood. Pass Middle Street Farm and its associated pond, before re-crossing the railway, via the bridge. The road curves around to the right, with another rhyne coming alongside on your left. Eventually the road bends back sharply left and takes you past Elm View and other properties, towards the end-junction with the main road. Turn right along the road for about 150 metres. At Exeter House, just before

the bend/junction, cross the road towards the field gate and footpath sign. (You can detour here along Brent Street to the Red Cow; the pub is about 300 metres along, on the left.)

G Take the gate and follow the hedged/ fenced path. Go through the following gate into the sloping field – up which you steeply climb some of the way back up Brent Knoll. At the top take the stile, to reach a plateau. Turn left along the crossing path hedged/ fenced path. Continue through an incomplete stile and the following gate. Follow along, as the path bends sharp right around the water treatment plant. Exit via the next stile, into the field beyond. Follow the left-hand hedge for about 50 metres and take the small gate. Bear left along the next field to exit via the gate in the far hedgerow. Proceed in a similar direction through the four subsequent fields, via various gates and stiles. The spire of East Brent church becomes increasingly evident ahead. Take the stile into the fifth field. The waymarking is misleading at this point. You must bear right and downhill, across the valley, to enter the scrubland ahead. Take the stile/footbridge. Follow the path on a short climb through the scrubland. Emerge, at the top, into the adjacent field, in which you follow along the left-hand hedgerow, to the stile adjacent to the field gate ahead. Turn left along the road. After about 50 metres, take the gate off to the right leading into the field overlooking the church. Go down to the bottom of the field, boundary right, and take the gate into the churchyard. Follow the path through the extended graveyard. Take the small gate off to the right, into the main churchyard. Turn left alongside the church, to reach the main entrance. Exit back on to Church Road. A

No. 7

Queen Charlton, Keynsham and Compton Dando

Distance 8.5 miles / 14 kms

Time 4 hours

OS Map Explorer 155

Starting Point Village green, outside St Margaret's Church, Queen Charlton – OS reference 634671

Parking Free off-road parking; at a triangle adjacent to Queen Charlton Lane, the road leading into Queen Charlton from the A37. The parking area is off to the right about 200 metres before you reach the built-up area of the village. There are some limited on-road opportunities in the village nearer to the church – please park responsibly

Reaching the start from Bristol Go out of Bristol on the A37, for about six miles. On the edge of the built-up area of Bristol, at Whitchurch village, take the road, off to the left, signed for Keynsham and Queen Charlton. Almost immediately, turn left again, to take the lesser lane signed to Queen Charlton. Proceed for about two miles. Just as Queen Charlton appears ahead, look out for the parking area off to the right

Refreshments Various options in Keynsham; or the Compton Inn, Compton Dando

---

A VARIED WALK exploring the Chew Valley via the interesting town of Keynsham and the attractive villages of Queen Charlton, Compton Dando and Woollard. The route follows along riverbanks, field paths and tracks, plus a little road walking. A few short climbs, with some wet and muddy stretches.

The walk starts from Queen Charlton and proceeds along the valley of Charlton Bottom; before turning uphill through Keynsham, passing via the town centre to the Memorial Park. From here, the walk follows along the River Chew, using a substantial section of the Two Rivers Way, to reach Compton Dando. The route then deviates uphill through woodland and across fields to Woollard; from where there is a climb and a further passage across fields. After going through further woodland, you turn sharply up an old byway, which eventually morphs into Highway Lane; from which you enjoy panoramic views across the Chew Valley, as you return to Queen Charlton.

A The walk starts outside St Margaret's church. With your back to the church gates and the village green over to your left, follow the no-through road straight ahead, immediately past Tolzey House. Take the gate at the end, to enter the following field. Bear left and downhill, to take the gate in the wooded corner. Cross the stream via the footbridge, to enter the copse. As the paths diverge, twice keep left, to follow along the left-hand fence within the copse. Eventually emerge into the field and proceed up the left-hand hedgerow, to the top corner.

Exit via the gate, to enter a wild open area. With the valley floor obvious down to the left, keep straight ahead along the valley side, ignoring any immediate temptation to descend fully. Keep with this path for about 900 metres, as it gradually descends and curves gently to the right. Go ahead through the gate in the hedgerow. Briefly pass through scrubland and, upon emerging, continue ahead along the valley bottom, through more wild meadow. Keep alongside the scrubland. Continue straight ahead over the crossing path, past the waymark post.

Within about a further 100 metres re-enter scrubland. Continue through the gate and in the same direction, passing the pond over to your left. Exit the scrubland via the next gate, into further wild meadow. Keep with the left-hand hedge and up the meadow. At the top corner take another gate into the following field. Go left and down the field; turn right at the bottom and walk with the stream on your left. In the far corner, ignore the footbridge and take the metal gate beyond. Go straight through the adjoining field and another gate. Immediately turn sharp right, through the further gate and into the paddock. Climb the hillside, with the hedge on your right, to the top. Take the gate, climb the fenced path, through trees and up steps to an estate road on the edge of Keynsham.

B Turn left down the estate road. Pass Broadlands Academy and continue to the crossroads. Keep straight ahead into Culvers Road and follow it uphill for about 100 metres. As Culvers Road curves away to the right, keep straight ahead into St John's Court, the no-through-road. Pass Tesco and towards the end of the cul-de-sac, turn left through the garage court. Pick up the crossing path and turn right, to follow it, via the walled passage, to the road at the end. Cross and turn left, to approach Keynsham High Street. With the church opposite turn right and through the main roundabout. Continue along the High Street, go over the zebra crossing and follow along the left-hand pavement. Just after entering the traffic-managed section of the HIgh Street, take the walled path off to the left, signed for the Memorial Park. Follow the path into the gardens, turn right along the crossing path and pass the ice cream parlour. At the playground entrance turn sharp left and weave downhill through the gardens, to reach the valley bottom in front of the bandstand.

C Turn right along the near bank of the River Chew – this is your direction now for a long stretch. Continue through the underpass, beneath the main road. Cross the footbridge, with ornamental ponds on the right. Follow the tarmac path through woodland into the short cul-de-sac ahead. At the T-junction, with Chew Cottage ahead, turn right and then left at the junction that immediately follows. Walk ahead to Albert Mill, which has been converted into flats. Obey the footpath signs as they direct you up to the right and through the courtyard and then left through the passageway, to emerge by the restored waterwheel. Follow the path along the riverside, past the millrace and through the copse. Take the gate into the following field. Keep along the riverbank. Pass through this and the three following fields, via further gates or gaps in the hedgerow. In the field beyond, with woodland ahead, keep alongside the fence that appears on the right. Take the field gates ahead, passing through two small enclosures on what can be a very muddy track. Exit, via the gate at the end. Join the road ahead and keep straight ahead for about 50 metres. Turn left, to take the gate into the adjacent field. You are now back alongside the river, with Chewton Place on the opposite bank. Cross the footbridge and continue straight ahead along the field, keeping towards the river and passing just to the left of an electricity pole. Take the wide gate/bridge/gate into the narrow field ahead. Exit, via the gate and cross the track with a bridge over to your left. Keep ahead through the gate opposite and into the large field that follows. Continue in the same direction, to cross the footbridge and take the gate into the following field. The path continues to

meander with the river. You eventually take the left-hand gate, following which you temporarily diverge from the river. Head diagonally up the field, to take the gate at the top. Immediately turn left at the junction, to go downhill towards woodland. Cross the bridge and take the gate into the woodland. Proceed along the fenced path, passing through another gate. Take the gate at the end into the following field. Briefly continue alongside the woodland edge, beyond which the field opens up and the river becomes evident again down to your left. Keep ahead in the same direction across the remainder of the field and exit via the gate. Keep alongside the river and through the next field. Exit via the following gate, to enter newly planted woodland. Keep ahead on the broad fenced path through the woodland, all the way to the village of Compton Dando.

D On reaching the road at Compton Dando, exit via the gate. Turn left across the bridge and towards the village centre. Up to the right there is an attractive view of St Mary the Blessed Virgin. Carry on to the Compton Inn. Opposite the Inn turn right up Church Lane. Bend right with the lane, to enter the churchyard. Pass through to the right of the church, and exit on the other side via steps. Head towards the Old Mill. Follow the path in front of and around the building and then between two ponds. Take the gate and follow the fenced path through the paddock area, now back alongside the River Chew. Cross the stile/footbridge/stile over the river. Bear slightly left across the meadow, to take the gate into the woodland ahead. Keep uphill and slightly left, staying within the left-hand boundary all the way, up to the top. Take the gate, to emerge from the woodland and into the adjacent field. Go up the wide fenced footpath, as panoramic views open up beyond. Descend to the left-hand corner, to exit via the gate into the next field. Walk down the centre and through the gap. Continue in the same direction, up and along the following field. Descend, via the gate, into the copse ahead. Go down through the copse, keeping to the left-hand fence. As you emerge the village of Woollard appears ahead. Follow the track across the stream and wild meadow. Keep along the meadow, to take the field gate at the far end. Follow the hedged/walled track gently uphill, to reach the T-junction with the road. (It is worth briefly detouring into the village, by turning left and left again, to reach the scenic bridge across the river.)

E To continue the walk: turn right at the T-junction. Proceed steeply up the road, passing Langford Farm. Towards the top of the hill, turn left and continue for about 50 metres to reach the crossing road. Take the gate hidden in the hedgerow immediately opposite the junction and 70 meters from the power line. Enter the field and bear slightly left

across it, beneath the power lines. Exit via the gate in the far hedgerow. Cross the footbridge, take the following gate and emerge, through brambles, into the next field. Proceed hedge left. Ignore the first gate. Continue ahead to take the gate in the left-hand corner. In the following field keep with the left-hand hedge. Go through the gate and across the footbridge, into the next field. Follow the left-hand hedge all the way down this long field, to the far corner. Take the track through the field gate into the woodland ahead. Cross the stream as best you can. Go uphill on the other side and, in about 50 metres, take the metal gate ahead. About 20 metres beyond there is a waymark post at the junction of several paths. Follow straight ahead. Continue uphill for about 150 metres. Take the stile in the corner, to exit the woodland and enter the paddock. Bear diagonally up the paddock to take the stile in the far left-hand corner. Cross the stable-yard and exit, via the gate, onto the road. Turn right up the minor road and continue, for about 100 metres, to the crossroads immediately beyond 'Greenfields'.

F At the crossroads turn right and up the by-way. Continue steeply up this hedged lane, passing several properties over to the left. The lane becomes surfaced at its top end, as you near the crossing road. Go straight across the busy road, to take Highwalls Lane, immediately opposite. Follow this hedged lane, from which there are long panoramic views, for the remainder of the walk. As you gradually descend back towards Queen Charlton, the church tower becomes increasingly evident. A track merging in from the right signals that you have almost reached the recommended parking area. If you have parked elsewhere, continue straight ahead on the road towards the village centre. **A**

No. 8

Burrington Combe, Velvet Bottom and Beacon Batch

Distance 10.5 miles / 17 kms

Time 4.5 to 5 hours

OS Map Explorer 141

Starting Point Public car park near to the bottom of Burrington Combe on the B3134, immediately adjacent to the Burrington Inn – OS reference 476588

Parking Free car parking

Reaching the start from Bristol Go south on the A38. Pass Bristol Airport. Just over half-a-mile beyond the Holiday Inn, take the minor road off to the left, signed to Burrington. Turn right at the T-junction with the A368. Ignore the first road off to the left signed to Burrington village. Take the second turning soon afterwards. Proceed up Burrington Combe until, just beyond the Burrington Inn, you reach a public car park to the left

Refreshments Burrington Inn, Burrington Combe

THIS CHALLENGING, BUT HIGHLY REWARDING, circle samples the varied landscapes in the heart of the Mendip Hills Area of Outstanding Natural Beauty (AONB) – including Burrington Combe, Velvet Bottom, Black Down and Beacon Batch, the highest point on Mendip. The route passes through several nature reserves, including various flora and fauna. There are a few prolonged climbs and one slightly tricky descent.

The walk starts towards the foot of Burrington Combe, from which it climbs to and across the plateau of Burrington Ham. After traversing the ancient Luvers Lane, the route steadily progresses further uphill towards the elevated wireless station. There follows a gentle descent to Charterhouse. Passing disused mine workings, you traverse the unusual terrain of Velvet Bottom. Near to Black Rock Gate, the route joins the West Mendip Way – and climbs through Long Wood and across exposed fields towards Tyning's Gate. There follows a further climb on to Black Down and Beacon Batch. The walk descends towards the southern edge of Burrington Combe – and follows down along it. The walk concludes with a sharp descent back into the combe, passing the famous Rock of Ages before returning to the car park opposite.

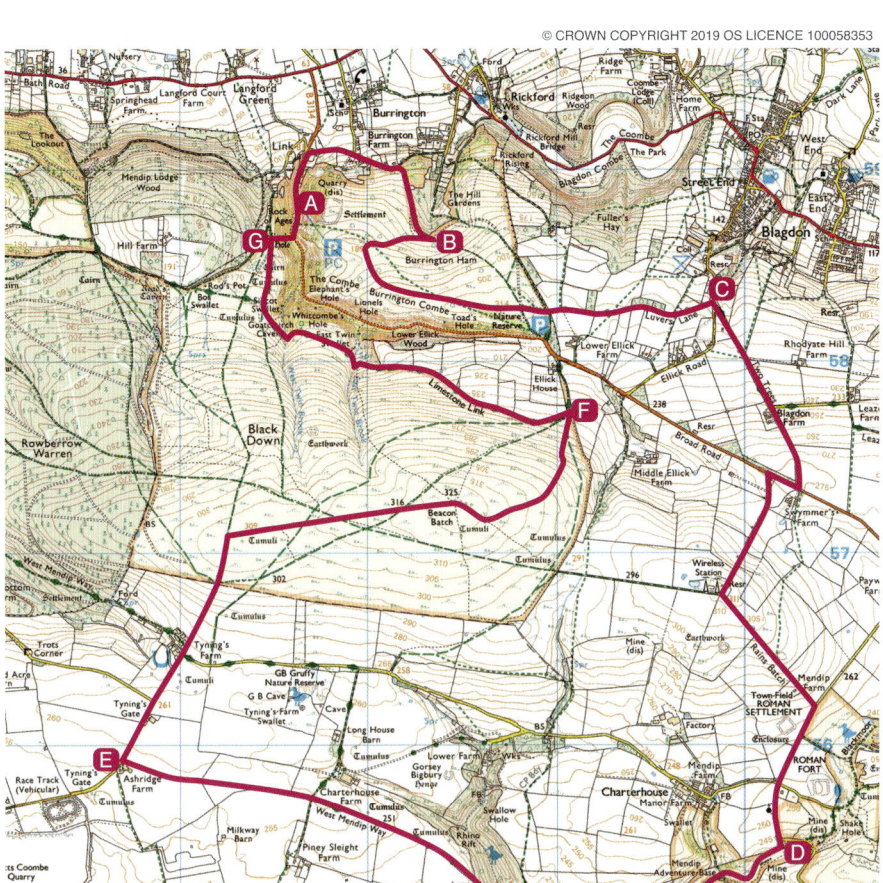

© CROWN COPYRIGHT 2019 OS LICENCE 100058353

A Exit the car park via the pedestrian gate, next to the AONB information board and public toilets, to enter the curtilage of the Burrington Inn. Pass through the garden area and car park – and all the way along the frontage of the inn. Follow the footway down the verge of Burrington Combe. At the road junction turn right, to take Ham Link. Continue uphill passing various houses and turns off to the left and right. When you reach the sign 'unsuitable for motors' keep on ahead as the road becomes more of a driveway. At the top of the rise and immediately opposite to The Hames, turn right through the gate and into the woodland. Keep ahead up the well-defined path. At the waymarked fork keep straight ahead. As the gradient lessens you reach the waymarked T-junction with a crossing track.

B At the junction turn sharp right. Proceed gradually up the track until you exit the woodland and encounter a stony outcrop, Long Rock. After a detour to

45

enjoy the panoramic views, continue on the same track as it initially curves away to the left. After about 50 metres take the right-hand fork. This grassy track soon bends leftwards, up on to the plateau of Burrington Ham. Keep straight ahead on the well-defined track; it eventually meets a wider waymarked track merging from the left. Keep ahead until you reach a major crossroads of tracks. Go straight ahead on the defined path across the open common land – to the Burrington Ham edge of the perimeter. Exit via the gate into the adjacent field. Keep to the right-hand hedge and pass through the gap. Carry on through two further fields, in the same direction along the right-hand hedgerow, passing a short stretch of woodland. Continue through the field gate as the track, Luvers Lane, becomes tarmacked and enclosed. Keep ahead, all the way down to the road junction.

C At the junction take Rhodyate/Two Trees, the furthest away of the two roads leading up to the right. This is a steady climb of almost 1000 metres, up a long straight road. After passing Hill Farm on your right, you eventually reach the T-junction with the B3134. Turn right and proceed carefully along the main road for just over 150 metres. Immediately beyond Swymmer's Cottage turn left, up the hedged green lane. Continue uphill, to approach the wireless station at the top of the hill. Take the gate and proceed to the junction of tracks. Turn left adjacent to the covered reservoir, and go downhill on the tarmacked track. At the T-junction at the bottom, turn right along the crossing road. Keep straight ahead for about 700 metres, passing the remains of the Roman settlement on your left. Go through the crossroads and past the Mendip Hills AONB Outdoor Activity Centre and St Hugh's church. From here, the road curves left and descends towards Velvet Bottom. As you approach the valley bottom take the short-cut down the right-hand verge, through brambles, to reach the crossing track. If you prefer you can take the longer route down the road to pick up the start of the track.

D Turn right along the track, to take the gate. You enter Velvet Bottom, a Site of Special Scientific Interest (SSSI) noted for its flora and fauna, and also with a history of lead mining dating back to Roman times. Descend gently on the surfaced/grass path all the way along Velvet Bottom, for at least 1500 metres in all. Eventually you exit via the gate at the end, to arrive at a junction near to Black Rock Gate. Turn right and uphill. After about 100 metres, go through the gate, to enter Long Wood, another SSSI/Nature Reserve. Follow the track uphill through the woodland. At the top, exit via the gate into the following field. Keep alongside the left-hand boundary wall/fence throughout this exceptionally long field. Exit via the gate, cross the farm track and take the gate opposite. Continue through the next field, still boundary left. Go through the following gate and into the following field. Keep ahead in the same direction – initially along the left-hand boundary – then aim for the gate at the right-hand end of the line of trees with farm buildings beyond. Go through the gate, to reach the picnic area immediately on your left. Continue through the field, along the right-hand boundary and through Ashridge Farm. Exit via the gate on to the road.

E Turn right and go straight ahead along the road, passing through the junction. At Tyning's Farm leave the road and keep straight ahead on the track. Climb steeply up the fenced track. Exit via the gate at the top, to enter the perimeter of

Black Down – another SSSI and also an Ancient Monument, both on account of Bronze Age barrows – and tumps made as a decoy to deflect air attacks on Bristol during the Second World War. Initially keep ahead in the same direction. After about 250 metres, however, look out for the low waymark in the ground. Turn right, to take the identified track. On a clear day you can see the path running in a straight uphill, towards the top of Beacon Batch. The first stretch of the path can be muddy – as you progress, though, the surface markedly improves. Continue in the straight-line, crossing several other tracks to reach the trig-point for Beacon Batch, the highest point on Mendip, from which there are spectacular views. Keep straight ahead on the same path, in the same direction, down Beacon Batch. Initially keep on an alignment just to the right of the two towers of the wireless station you passed earlier in the walk, on the horizon ahead.

At the first fork – about 200 metres beyond the trig point – turn left, to take the initially broad, ill-defined track. The route gradually becomes clearer as you proceed downhill in the direction of Chew Valley Lake in the distance below. Blagdon Lake moves into view, as you descend further. Towards the bottom of the slope, stick with the main track as it bends gently towards the edge of the Black Down perimeter. You reach a waymark post, just within the perimeter boundary, identifying the junction of several paths.

F Turn left, to take the path running alongside the right-hand boundary of the Black Down perimeter. Almost immediately bear right at the fork, to ensure that you remain just within the boundary. You now keep in this same general direction, in parallel with Burrington Combe, for about 2000 metres. At first the path rises gradually.

Soon the terrain levels out and then you begin to descend again. Keep ahead with the path, as it descends more steeply and in and out of pockets of scrubby woodland. As you proceed there are occasional glimpses across and into Burrington Combe. Enter a more extensive copse, cross the stream and stay with the track as it curves right and uphill, to exit into open land again. Initially bend left and uphill with the track, keeping towards the edge of Burrington Combe. As you plateau and begin to descend again, avoid straying too far off to the right. Keep straight ahead on the main path, down through further scrubland. Cross another stream to join the crossing track. Turn right and continue briefly uphill, for about a further 50 metres.

G At the waymark, take the right-hand path leading downhill through bracken. Descend steeply into the woodland, soon picking up again the route of the stream you just crossed. Re-cross the stream as you near the bottom. Carry on along the other side. Descend steps to cross the stream again. Continue along the stream. Re-cross yet again to pick up the track alongside. Cross the stream for one last time and then descend the track back into Burrington Combe. At the road, turn left and follow the adjacent path as it weaves in and out of woodland for about 200 metres in all. You reach the Rock of Ages ahead. Allegedly this was the inspiration for the hymn of the same name, written by local curate Augustus Montague Toplady, in 1763. Cross the road to reach the car park opposite, from which you started the walk. **A**

No. 9

Fretherne, Arlingham and Saul

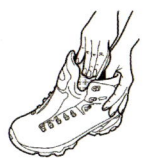

Distance 10.5 miles / 17 kms

Time 5 hours

OS Map Explorer OL14

Starting Point Sandfield Bridge, Church Lane, to the south-east of the centre of Saul – OS reference 754090

Parking Limited free parking alongside Church Lane – the best opportunities may be to the south-east of Sandfield Bridge, near to the Oatfield junction. Otherwise use the pay and display car park, immediately to the north-east of Sandfield Bridge

Reaching the start from Bristol Go north on the M5. Exit by Junction 13. Turn left on the A419 and then left again on to the A38. Almost immediately take the B4071, off to the right. Proceed for over a mile, to reach the central green of Frampton-on-Severn. Turn right along Whitminster Lane and proceed to the edge of Frampton/Oatfield. Take a left-hand turning, Church Lane, which is signed to Saul

Refreshments The Old Passage Inn, Arlingham (or detour via the Red Lion); or the Ship Inn, Upper Framilode; or the Stables Café at the start/finish; or seats suitable for picnics

---

THIS WALK CIRCLES the Arlingham horseshoe, a peninsula within a deep meander of the River Severn, immediately opposite to Newnham and the Forest of Dean (see Walk 11) with which it was once connected by ford and ferry. Most of this very level walk follows the Severn Way, with the towpaths of the Gloucester and Sharpness Canal and the (abandoned) Stroudwater Canal providing the linking section.

The walk starts on the Gloucester and Sharpness Canal. You soon turn past Saul Lodge, to join the Severn Way and follow along the riverbank. You go through woodland and pass near Arlingham, before reaching the Old Passage Inn directly opposite to Newnham, from where the ferry once ran. You continue around the horseshoe through Arlingham Warth, with Westbury-on-Severn and Garden Cliff opposite, and on through Priding towards Framilode church. You deviate from the river, to take the disused Stroudwater Canal, which you follow to its junction with the main Gloucester and Sharpness Canal. From here, it is only a short distance back to Sandfield Bridge.

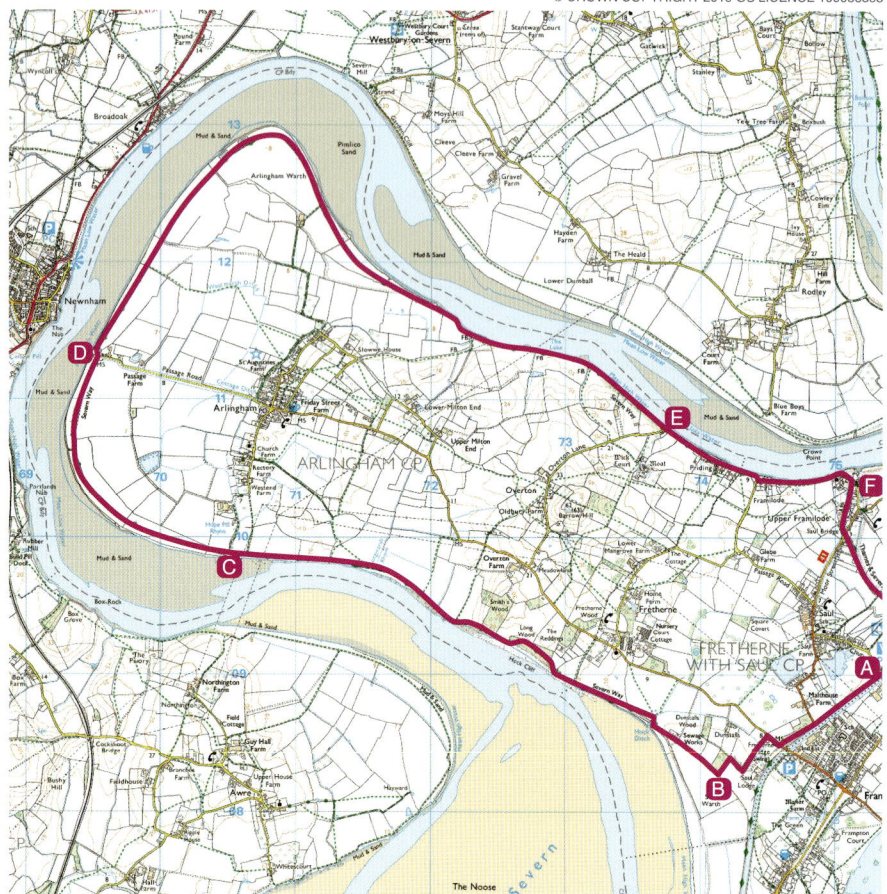

A Start from Sandfield Bridge on the Saul side of the Gloucester and Sharpness Canal, facing westwards. Turn left alongside the canal. After about 500 metres exit, via the gate, to reach Fretherne swing bridge. Cross the road and turn right. After about 50 metres, fork left on the road signposted towards Arlingham and Fretherne. Proceed along the left-hand side for about 100 metres. Beyond the frontage of the cottage turn left along the track. With Saul Lodge and its grounds over to the left, carry on along the wooded/fenced track. Do not take the field gate ahead. Instead, take the stile off to the right and go into scrubby woodland. Beware of the holes arising from badger setts along this stretch. Keep alongside the left-hand boundary for about 100 metres. Take the stile in the left-hand fence to enter the adjacent field. Cross the field, alongside the woodland, to the right-hand corner.

B Climb the low fence to enter the next field. The official fenced route of the footpath runs immediately off to the right – but has become overgrown and fallen into disuse. Instead, advance into the field for about 5 metres and then

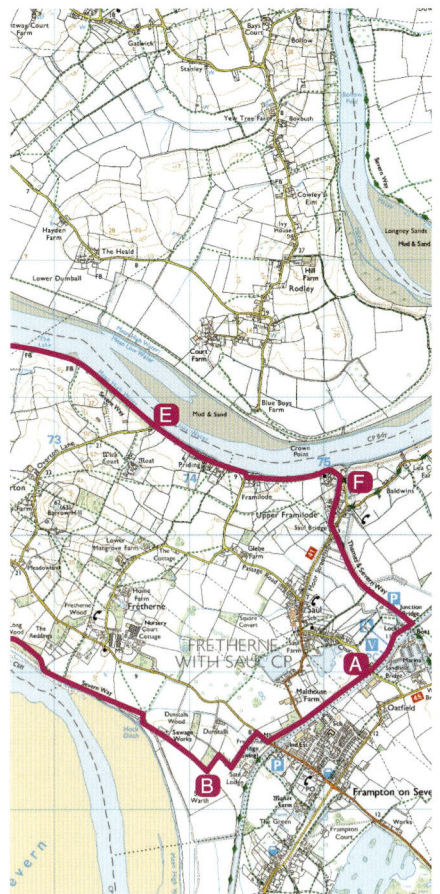

turn sharp right, to follow along the outer edge of the official route. Keep towards the edge of the field throughout, aiming for the field gate in the far corner. Exit via the gate and proceed straight ahead up on to the raised track, servicing the sewage works. Turn left and head towards the river. On reaching the river embankment, you now simply turn right and follow it up-river. Soon deviate slightly to take the signposted diversion, via the footbridge, at the sluice gate. Return immediately to the riverbank, from which there are panoramic views down the estuary and towards The Noose sandbank, where legend says that a Roman legion was drowned by the incoming tide. Soon you pick up the left-hand fence ahead. Continue, via stiles/footbridges/gates, through successive fields. With a house, the Reddings, immediately over to your right, take the gate into Long Wood. Proceed through the wood and exit, via another gate, into the following field. Follow along the left-hand hedge to take the stile/footbridge/stile into Smith's Wood ahead. Exit, via the further gate, into the next field with spectacular views ahead towards Arlingham, Newnham and the Forest of Dean. Carry on down the left-hand hedge and soon take the raised embankment, which affords elevated views of the river once again. Keep ahead along the embankment, by the river. Pass through seven gates in all, before reaching the second of two prominent pylons carrying power lines over the River Severn. There is a notice board at this point containing a useful map of the whole 'horseshoe peninsula'. Upon passing through another gate and across the rhyne, you reach the junction with a track turning off to the right offering access to the village of Arlingham (a diversion of about 500 metres to the Red Lion pub, in the village centre).

C To continue along the main route from the junction: keep straight ahead through the immediate gate. Follow the river through open land, with the river slightly more distant but the dyke continuing to provide elevated views. Ever closer views materialise of Bullo and Newnham, over on the other side of the river. Carry on through a total of five more gates. The path curves around the

horseshoe, until you take one more gate, to reach the Old Passage Inn. You can rest at the seat on the riverbank, near to the point from which the ferry ran for many years until the late 1940s connecting with Newnham opposite.

D Take the metal gate to exit Old Passage. Continue along the footpath on top of the embankment, through three further gates, heading in the general direction of the prominent Westbury-on-Severn church tower, also on the other side of the river. As you curve around the next bend of the horseshoe, you come on to Arlingham Warth. You pass through another gate, with the prominent Garden Cliff now opposite. Continue along the embankment via two more gates to take the stile, immediately beyond which stands a prominent 'Severn Way' waymark. Proceed along the embankment and through two further gates. Pass the stables complex over to the right. Take the gate into the next field, and keep ahead to reach a further prominent pylon taking cables across the river. Immediately beyond the pylon, take the stile/footbridge/stile and keep straight ahead into the following field. Stick to the left-hand edge, alongside the brush. In the far boundary, take the gate/footbridge/gate. Go through another gate and follow the narrow, fenced track along the left-hand edge of the next field. Take the following gate, as the track widens and diverges down from the field. The track becomes increasingly muddy, as it traverses a long strip of grazing land. Pass through two more gates. Eventually exit via the gate up in the far right-hand corner, and on to the road adjacent to a cottage.

E Continue straight ahead along the road for about 800 metres, and through the riverside hamlet of Priding. Keep

with the road as it turns sharply right, to reach the edge of the dispersed settlement of Framilode. Immediately turn left along the cul-de-sac, still parallel with the river. Continue to the end and take the footpath through the archway in the hedge ahead. Carry on along the fenced footpath until you reach the stile and gate side-by-side. Take the (left-hand) gate and follow the riverbank for about a further 200 metres. On reaching the barrier at the end, climb the steps on to the access road in front St Peter's Church, Framilode. Take the road and follow it as it bends away from the river. No more than 100 metres beyond the church and opposite to the post box, you cross a (not immediately obvious) bridge over the reed-choked Stroudwater Canal, which once linked the Severn with Stroud.

F Immediately beyond the bridge turn right along the canal towpath. After passing the backs of various houses of Upper Framilode, you soon come across The Ship Inn. Beyond here, continue beside the canal to reach the road at Saul Bridge. Cross the road and keep ahead, along the hedged/fenced path, still beside the canal. As another channel merges in from the left, stick with the path, which from here onwards runs along the right-hand side of the canal. After you have crossed a total of six stiles, Wycliffe College Boat Club appears on the horizon ahead. This marks the junction of the Stroudwater Canal, along which you are now walking, with the main Gloucester and Sharpness Canal, on which you started the walk. Proceed up to the junction and turn right, along the surfaced towpath of the main canal. Pass the Cotswold Canals Trust visitor centre, the toilets and the Stables Café, to return to the starting point, Sandfield Bridge. **A**

No. 10
Shirenewton, Llanmelin Fort and Itton Common

Distance 8 miles / 13 kms
Time 4 to 4.5 hours
OS Map Explorer OL14
Starting Point Recreation ground, Shirenewton – OS reference 476937
Parking Free car parking at the recreation ground
Reaching the start from Bristol Go west on the M4. Exit by Junction 21 to take the M48 over the Severn Bridge. Exit by Junction 2, then on to the A466 towards Chepstow. Go over the major roundabout in the direction of, but not as far as, the racecourse. Continue downhill for about half-a-mile. Prior to reaching the next roundabout, take the left-hand turn along the B4235, signed to Usk. Continue for about three miles then turn sharp left and uphill for Shirenewton. Upon reaching the village centre, turn right at the T-junction, signed to Earlswood and Usk. Continue towards the edge of the village to reach the recreation ground, which is signed off to the left
Refreshments Tredegar Arms, Shirenewton; or Carpenters Arms, Mynydd-bach

---

THIS UNDULATING WALK explores the countryside overlooking the Severn Estuary to the west of Chepstow. It encompasses the attractive village of Shirenewton, an interesting Iron Age fort, a secluded coombe and various panoramic views, including of both bridges across the Severn. There is a short, steep descent from the fort ideally requiring the assistance of a walking-pole, and an alternative route, easily avoiding this.

Starting at Shirenewton, the walk progresses westwards along country lanes and then up through woodland to Llanmelin Fort. There follows a brief, steep descent into The Coombe, which you follow along until climbing steeply up to the hamlet of Argoed. The route follows tracks and paths through various farms and across the B4235 down into Coed Llifos valley. You progress around the head of the valley, before turning back along it and uphill to Itton Common. There are spectacular views across the Estuary as you proceed along Itton Hill and down towards Mynydd-bach. The route finally ascends through an open buffer area, separating the adjacent villages. Upon reaching Shirenewton again, you return, via the main square, to the start.

A Exit from the car park back on to the road. Cross and turn right, towards the centre of Shirenewton. At the crossroads opposite to the Tredegar Arms, turn right and up in the direction of the church of St Thomas a Becket. After about 100 metres and opposite to the church, bear right to take the waymarked stile/field gate ahead. This leads you on to a short, enclosed track through the following field gate and into the paddock ahead. Bear diagonally right, to take the stile down in the far right-hand corner. Cross the road and take the gate immediately opposite into the following field. Within about 30 metres bear right, to take the gate in the right-hand corner. Cross the driveway in front of the main gates of Home Farm, a stables complex. Take the gate into the large field. Proceed all the way down the right-hand boundary. Exit via the pedestrian gate on to the road. Turn left and continue downhill, with panoramic views opening up across to the Severn Estuary and beyond. At the no-through-road, keep right and shortly left to continue down the same road. Coombe Farm becomes ever more obvious, over to your right. The road descends to reach the farm driveway, immediately opposite to which is a track leading off to the left.

B Take the track into the woodland. View the Cadw sign about the Iron Age Llanmelin Fort, which you are about to visit. Follow the track straight uphill for about 50 metres, to reach the edge of the adjacent field. Turn right within the woodland, to follow the waymarked path along the field edge. The increasingly clear path curves left and right, as you proceed uphill through the woodland. Eventually, you emerge, via the field gate/stile, on to the fort. Keep straight ahead. You may wish to explore the earthworks further, before returning to the main path. The descent ahead is steep, but with due care reasonably straightforward. (If you are without a walking-pole, however, I recommend a short detour. Retrace your footsteps – the way you ascended. Then, turn left along the road, to rejoin the route, just before **C**). To resume on the preferred route: keep straight ahead on the main path to reach the fort perimeter. Turn right, down the path, between the ramparts and the further woodland. At the very obvious corner, exit the fort curtilage via the stile straight ahead, to go back into the woodland. Proceed cautiously as you descend, sometimes steeply, on what is mostly a well-defined path. The path initially bears leftwards but eventually curves back around to the right, along and down the embankment.

At the bottom you turn right, to join the crossing track, along the valley and next to the stream. You soon exit the woodland and rejoin the road you were on previously. Turn left along the road. Cross the stream to reach the junction.

C Turn right along The Cwm following the stream. You keep along this quiet wooded valley for about 1200 metres in all. Pass the waterfall and The Cwm (a house) on your right. Keep with the road as it crosses the stream and goes slightly uphill, ignoring a path off to the right. The road crosses the river again before you reach Maes-y-Gwenith on your left. Here, go straight across the further bridge to cross the stream yet again. Do not, however, follow the road any further.

D Beyond the bridge take the field gate immediately ahead, to enter the sloping field. Advance up the right-hand boundary. In the corner, take the field gate/stile to enter the woodland ahead. Climb steeply up the track, between the fence and the tributary stream. When you emerge from the woodland go over a crossing track and take the field gate immediately ahead. Keep straight ahead up the following field, to take the field gate in the far boundary. Enter the spinney and bear left up the track, to exit via the further field gate. Enter the adjacent field, within which you keep alongside the right-hand hedge, to exit via the gate on to the driveway, next to Lower Argoed. Continue up the driveway for no more than 50 metres, before taking the stile off to the left. Enter the field, which you cross, to take the stile in the boundary ahead. Continue uphill in a similar direction across the corner of the

next field. Exit via the stile in the hedgerow and cross the minor road. Go up the verge immediately opposite to take the stile into the next field. Keep up the right-hand boundary and cross the double stile. Bear slightly left up the following field. Exit via the field gate on to the road, opposite to Red House. With spectacular views down to the Severn Estuary, turn right along the road, for about 200 metres. At the junction, turn left. Continue along the main road for about 50 metres.

E Take the track leading up to the right, towards The Marls. Continue up the metalled bridleway past the farm and other buildings. Just beyond the Marls, as the metalled driveway deviates sharply away to the left, continue straight ahead down the unsurfaced bridleway. Keep ahead on this hedged green lane as it bends leftwards and further downhill, until reaching the B4235. Cross the B road and advance down the surfaced no-through-road opposite. Pass three properties and continue as the road morphs into the driveway of Pant-y-Cosyn farm and curves left towards it. Pass to the left of the main farmhouse. Cross the stream and go through the field gate. Keep ahead up the short green lane and, through another gate, into the following field. Proceed on the sunken track alongside the left-hand hedge of the field. Exit via the stile into the next field. Keep to the left-hand boundary. Go through two successive field gates, passing the barn over to the right. In the next field, continue along the left-hand boundary. Take successive field gates to exit on to the road.

F Turn right and down the minor road. Continue, as the road passes Whitebrook Farm and meanders down towards the stream. Cross the bridge and pass the lake over to the left. Climb back uphill to reach the crossroads, where you turn right. In about a further 200 metres keep

straight ahead at the fork. Follow the road as it undulates along the hillside. At the multiple junction of roads/tracks, again keep straight ahead. You pass the entrance to Coed-Ilifos Farm, situated down to your right. Continue gradually downhill on the same road, passing woodland on both your left and right. At the bottom of the hill and after crossing a stream, the road reaches a crossroads. Strike out across the extensive verge towards the waymark post in the hedgerow ahead.

G Take the stile into the field. Climb steeply uphill and through the field gateway. Continue half-right up the next field and look out for the stile hidden in the hedgerow ahead. Take the stile, go across the next, narrow field. Exit via the following stile. Cross the road and take the field gate opposite onto Itton Common. Follow the track ahead, soon picking up the right-hand boundary alongside Itton Common Wood. On reaching the corner of the field/woodland, take the pedestrian gate into the next field. Immediately turn right, to continue along the edge of the woodland. As you proceed the Severn Estuary and both of the bridges come into view again. Keep alongside the same woodland boundary, through this and two further fields, via stiles/gates. Continue in the same direction down the next, larger, field with Cottage Farm prominent ahead and down to your left. Exit via the gate. Keep left and down the next field, passing just to the left of the single tree in the middle of the field. Go through the next gate. In the field beyond continue in the same direction, down towards the right-hand corner and adjacent to further woodland, Roughets Wood. Take the further gate, and closely follow the boundary of this woodland as it curves around to the

right. Beyond the woodland you reach open land interspersed with trees. Follow the straight line of trees gently downhill to reach an electricity pole. From here continue downhill in broadly the same direction towards the woodland ahead – with the backcloth of the village of Mynnyd-bach. Your target is the stile – not easily decipherable from afar – which you take to enter the woodland. Cross the stream ahead, via the bridge. Exit the woodland on to a short track, which soon merges in with an access road. Climb steeply uphill to reach the main road with The Carpenters Arms immediately over to the right.

H To continue, cross the main road and take the hedged/walled footpath immediately ahead, signed to School Hill. Continue uphill to exit into a housing estate. Cross both of the roads. Go up the steps immediately ahead, and climb the fenced path. You emerge via further steps and the following gate, into the tract of open land separating the villages of Mynnydd-bach and Shirenewton. Fork diagonally left along to the far corner. Cross the stream via the bridge. Take the right-hand field gate into a continuation of the open land. Keep ahead on the clear path, with the stream on your right. Pass the seat and proceed to the gate ahead. Exit on to the crossing, fenced footpath. Turn left, go through the further gate and into the end of a cul-de-sac. Keep straight ahead to exit Tan House Court. On the main road, turn right and continue uphill. Bear right to reach the junction with the main square of Shirenewton, adjacent to the Tredegar Arms. From here turn right, to retrace your steps to the car park from which you started. **A**

No. 11
Newnham, Blaize Bailey and Bullo

Distance 10 miles / 16 kms
Time 5 hours
OS Map Explorer OL14
Starting Point Newnham, on the west bank of the River Severn – OS reference 693120
Parking Free public car park
Reaching the start from Bristol Go west on the M4. Exit by Junction 1 to take the M48. Exit by Junction 2 and follow the signs towards Chepstow. Turn right at the first roundabout. Pass Chepstow on the A48 and keep ahead, through Lydney and Blakeney, to reach Newnham. Follow the A48 through the town and downhill. As you approach the riverbank towards the far edge of the village, turn right on to Church Road for the car park
Refreshments The Black Pig Ale House and other facilities in Newnham; no options en route. A couple of stops with panoramic views, suitable for picnic stops, early and late in the walk

---

THE KEY THEME of this Forest of Dean walk, on the western bank of the River Severn, is stunning panoramic views over the river, particularly towards the Arlingham Peninsula, directly opposite (see Walk 9). The walk predominantly follows pleasant woodland tracks; and scenic field and riverside paths. The terrain is undulating, with a couple of steep climbs.

The walk starts from the riverside village of Newnham. You progress uphill through fields to enter the heart of the Forest – with notable views from Blaize Bailey. You then deviate southwards on a lengthy woodland trek, before descending steeply into a tributary valley and towards Two Bridges. There is a short climb, before crossing the A48 at Kingsland; followed by a more gradual and prolonged descent, back down towards the River Severn again. The route bends back northwards alongside the river, via attractive meadows, Box Grove and the port/shipyard of Bullo. The walk concludes with a climb through Newnham churchyard; and then down the High Street to the riverside starting point.

A From the riverside car park, go left up the main road for just over 50 metres. Cross the road and take the first turning, Unlawater Lane. Proceed up the lane, ignoring side roads. Opposite to The Barn House, take the gate off to the left into the adjacent field. Proceed along the left-hand fence to take the gate in the corner. Go through the playground to exit via the gate on the far side. Turn left, along the road to the T-junction. Turn right and up Hyde Lane. Proceed across the railway bridge and keep ahead at the junction just beyond, to reach Gibraltar Cottage.

B Take the left turn by the side of the house, up steps and through the gate. Walk straight up the field, aiming well to the right of the house ahead. Take the gate into the following field and continue uphill in the same direction, to reach a plateau. Proceed until reaching the gate over to the left, giving access to the lane. Exit, via the gate, and cross the lane diagonally. Follow the metalled driveway opposite, for about 200 metres. Just beyond the farm buildings keep straight ahead, to take the stile/gate into the following field. Initially, continue in the same direction towards the electricity pylon ahead; beyond which bear right and uphill towards another pylon in the top right-hand corner. Climb the left-hand stile to enter the adjacent, undulating field. Keep ahead, following along the edge of the woodland. Continue through the field gate and along the next field, exiting via the gap in the far corner. In the subsequent field, maintain the same direction beside the woodland to take the stile in the top right-hand corner. In the field beyond, go forward for about 30 metres and then turn sharp right, to take the grassy track leading up to the further stile.

C Take the stile into the adjacent field. Climb ahead, passing to the left of the farm buildings to reach the crossing track. Turn right and follow the track as it almost immediately bends sharply to the left and downhill, towards the field gate by a derelict cottage. Take the adjacent stile to enter woodland. As you pass another derelict cottage the track enters denser coniferous woodland. Keep ahead to cross a minor track, beyond which you climb just over 75 metres. Join the surfaced, crossing track and turn right along it. Within about 100 metres keep left and go steeply uphill. You soon reach the panoramic Blaize Bailey viewpoint – a highly suitable stop. Beyond here, continue uphill for about 75 metres more to reach a major junction.

D Turn sharp left along the initially level track. Stay on the track for about 2000 metres in all, ignoring several turns off to the left, as it gradually descends to reach a sharp right-hand bend. At the start of the bend, take the path leading off to the left into the woodland. After about 75 metres bear left, as waymarked, to take the stile in the left-hand fence. Exit the woodland into the large, sloping field. Walk all the way down the left-hand boundary to the corner. Pass the stile and turn right along the bottom boundary, beside the stream/fence/woodland. Continue in the same direction via stiles along three further fields. Take the field gate into the next field. Continue downhill to exit via the field gate on to the lane ahead. Turn left down the lane, cross the bridge and pass the cottage.

E About 50 metres beyond the cottage, take the stile off to the right. Cross the field to take the stile in the hedgerow ahead. In the next field continue on the same alignment, towards the gateway in the far left-hand corner. Take the adjacent stile and cut across the corner of the adjacent field to climb another stile, about 10 metres to the left of the gateway. Keep ahead in the subsequent field, staying parallel with the nearby stream. Take the further stile in the tree-lined boundary ahead. In the following field keep slightly left and towards the higher ground. Cross the tributary stream and climb another stile. In the field beyond continue along the nearby stream. Take the stile ahead, by the field gate, and proceed along the left-hand fence. Pass the bridge and after about 50 metres look out for the left-hand field gate leading up into the sloping field.

F Take the gate, follow the track up the hillside for about 50 metres and then turn, very sharply left and steeply, up the extensive field in the direction of a large tree. Pass just to the right of the tree and

continue in the same direction, to take the field gate in the top left-hand corner. Within the following large field, stick alongside the left-hand boundary all the way up to the top corner. Turn left through the field gate into the adjacent field. Keep to the right-hand boundary and continue uphill. Pass through the gateway and cross the narrow field. Exit, via the stile, on to the main A48. Cross the road and turn left along the metalled footway. Follow all the way along the boundary wall frontage of the first house, Shephard's Cottage. By an overgrown bus-stop at the far end, take the hidden walled/fenced footpath, running between the property boundaries. Proceed to the end of this path, which can become overgrown in summer months but should always be passable. Climb the stile on the left to exit into the large field. The way forward from here is not immediately obvious on the ground, nor does the OS map greatly assist. Head across the centre of the field, passing in front of the country house. Bear very slightly to the left of the prominent wind turbine beyond the far boundary. Take the stile in the hedgerow and head straight down the following field, passing between the farm sheds and the wind turbine. Keep straight ahead to take another stile in the far hedgerow. Continue down the next field, aiming just to the left of the farmhouse. Exit the field via the gateway in the boundary, to reach the driveway of Bledisloe Farm.

G Cross the driveway and go through the gate. With scrubland over to your

left, continue through the farmyard, past barns. Keep ahead along the farm track for about a further 75 metres to reach a junction. Turn right, ignoring the waymark indicating only the fork ahead. Keep alongside the left-hand boundary. Continue, as the track bends and passes through the gateway and into a very large, open field. Very occasionally it may even be necessary to divert all the way around the left-hand boundary, down towards the field gate at the bottom. Mostly, however, it is easy to progress up the centre of the field in the broad direction of two pairs of distant electricity pylons – each spanning the River Severn. Upon reaching the brow of the field you will see the metal field gate down in the far right-hand corner – head straight towards it. Take the gate and follow down the left-hand edge of the next field until reaching another field gate, by which you exit on to the road. Turn right, cross the railway bridge and continue for about a further 250 metres in all, to reach a driveway off to the left, opposite an electricity pylon.

H Turn left, cross the cattle grid and continue along the driveway through open land. When the driveway becomes bounded, stay on it for about a further 75 metres – until taking the stile in the fence off to the left, leading into the adjacent field. Bear half-right, towards the powerline pole and the River Severn below. Continue down the field on exactly the same alignment, to cross the hidden stile/footbridge/stile in the far boundary into the adjacent field. Turn left and keep near to the left-hand field boundary. Take the further stile/footbridge/stile ahead, passing over the stream. Bear slightly right across the next field, and exit via the stile in the hedgerow. Go up the following field, keeping with the right-hand fence/hedgerow. Take the stile to enter Box Grove. Descend through the woodland, cross the bridge and exit via the stile. In the next field bear slightly left, before keeping with the right-hand boundary. Head towards the field gate and pass through it to reach Bullo Pill. Bullo developed as a port for exporting coal and stone from the Forest of Dean in the 19th century. Trade gradually declined and the main dock finally closed in 1926.

1 Beyond the field gate descend the concrete slope alongside the industrial fencing. Cross the access road and continue along the fenced path, beside the millpond. Cross straight over the lane. Follow the narrow path up alongside the terrace of houses. Turn right on the crossing driveway and follow it along the rear of the houses. Keep towards the right-hand wall to emerge, via the ginnel, into an open area. At the entrance to Peacehaven ahead, take the adjacent pedestrian gate. Follow the hedged/fenced path running between the railway and river. The path passes through a gate into woodland. Follow the enclosed path through two further gates to exit into the field ahead. With the railway veering away to the left and glimpses of Newnham becoming ever more apparent, keep towards the right-hand fence. At the end of the field take the small gate next to the field gate. Follow the hedged track across the small stream to reach the A48 again. Exit via the gate next to Callow Cottage. Turn right, up the pavement,

towards St Peter's church. Take the gate into the churchyard and proceed steeply uphill. There are fine views across the Severn from this elevated position. Until the late 1940s, a ferry crossed the river, from just below the church to Passage Pill on the Arlingham side. Follow the path out of the church grounds and via the main gate on to the High Street. Carry on straight down the High Street. In due course you pass the Black Pig Ale House (behind the former Ship Inn), over to the left. When you reach Beeches Road, turn right and continue to the T-junction with Church Road. Turn left and further downhill. Within about 75 metres, you are back at the car park where you started. **A**

No. 12

Luckington, Littleton Drew and Alderton

Distance 8 miles / 13 kms

Time 3 to 3.5 hours

OS Map Explorer 168

Starting Point Opposite to Luckington Community School, on the village green, Luckington – OS reference 833840

Parking Free on-street parking, at or near to the village green

Reaching the start from Bristol Go east on the M4. Leave by Junction 18 and then go north on the A46. At the traffic lights at Old Sodbury, turn right, to take the B4040 Malmesbury road. Continue on the B4040 via Acton Turville and Luckington Road, to reach Luckington village centre

Refreshments The Old Royal Ship, Luckington

AN EASY, ALMOST LEVEL, WALK incorporating the attractive south Cotswolds villages of Luckington and Alderton. The route comprises a mixture of field paths, tracks and lanes, including a short section of the Roman Fosse Way. This is an ideal walk in April and May, when the wild flowers are at their best.

The walk starts at Luckington village green, from where you proceed towards the church and then deviate southwards along an attractive valley. You subsequently cross many fields and under the main railway line, to reach the hamlet of Littleton Drew. From here, you proceed along a series of wooded tracks. You pick up the route of the Fosse Way for a short distance. You then bear in the direction of Alderton, traversing several more fields, before going through the village and past the church. Your return to Luckington is via further fields and a short stretch of tarmac. The walk skirts Luckington Court and goes through the churchyard before returning to the village centre, on the same road by which you earlier exited the village.

© CROWN COPYRIGHT 2019 OS LICENCE 100058353

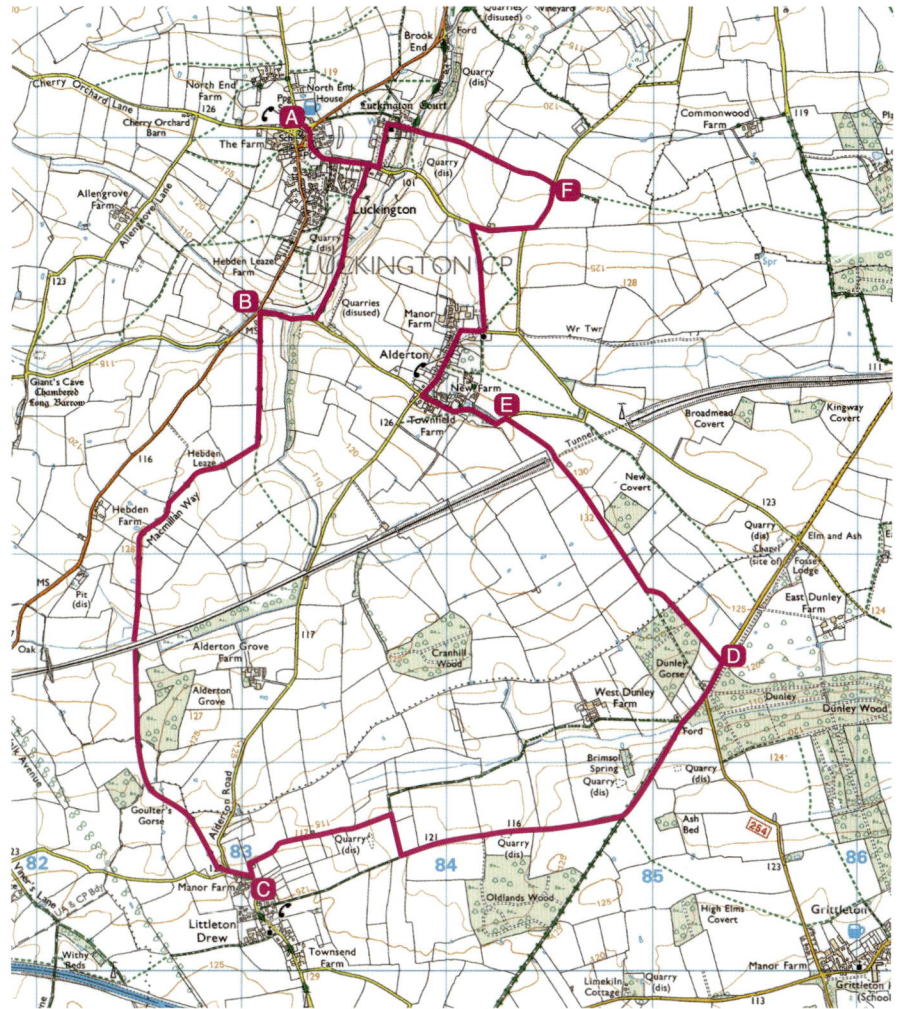

A From the primary school, take the road alongside the village green towards the recreation ground. Keep ahead at the junction, towards the church. Follow the right-hand pavement and gently descend Chapel Row/Church Road. After about 200 metres, just past the Old Smithy and opposite to Luckington Court, turn right along the enclosed footpath between properties. Take the stile into the field. Initially proceed parallel to the right-hand garden fence, but then bear slightly left, to take the wider gap in the hedgerow ahead, just to the right of a tree. In the next field, proceed along the top of the embankment. At the field end descend to take the gate down in the far left-hand corner. Enter the woodland and continue downhill, to cross the bridge over the stream. Exit the woodland into Tanhouse Meadow. Turn right to head along the valley. Follow the

69

stream towards the distant power pole, which you eventually go past. Take the gate in the hedgerow ahead. Turn right along the lane, until you near the T-junction with the main road.

B Just before the road junction, go through the gate off to the left to take the footpath. Proceed up the walled/hedged path, alongside Ashbourne House. Take the stile into the field ahead and continue along the left-hand hedgerow. Exit into the next field, via the gap in the hedgerow. Be careful as the precise route of the path at this point can be a little confusing. It is advisable to double-check with the map. Keep straight ahead into the field for about 200 metres, on the same alignment as before – parallel with, but not directly alongside, the left-hand hedgerow. From the centre of the field, strike out towards the obvious gap in the right-boundary hedgerow, situated about 100 metres from the far corner.

You should actually pass through a smaller, less obvious gap about 10 metres further to the right. Continue across the next field in the same direction, aiming for the waymark post at the corner of the spinney ahead. From here, keep ahead along the field edge for about 50 metres. At the field corner, cross the stone stile. Turn left across the next field, initially following the left-hand hedgerow and then continuing straight ahead towards the stile between two trees. Cross into the next field and bear half-right, to go through the field gate with an old brick kiln ahead in the distance. In the next field bear half-left, passing just to the left of the clump of trees encircling the fenced pond. Climb over the stile in the hedgerow beyond. In the following field, continue downhill towards the distant field gate situated on the front edge of the railway embankment, and leading into the underpass. Cross two small bridges over ditches, before taking the field gate. Go through the underpass and exit via another gate with the words 'Life is a Gift of God' inscribed upon its post. Enter the extensive field and bear slightly right across it towards two trees on the outer fringe of the woodland ahead. Bear further right, up the field towards the far corner of the woodland. Proceed along the woodland edge to take the gate into the following field. Keep ahead to take the large hedge gap, situated immediately to the left of further woodland. Follow the left-hand field boundary of the next field for about 100 metres, as it curves around – until taking the small gap in the left-hand hedgerow. Bear slightly right and down the following, narrow field, towards the field gate in the far hedgerow. Take the adjacent stile to enter the next field. Head diagonally right up this long field, with the hamlet of Littleton Drew increasingly evident ahead. About 50 metres ahead of the far corner of the field, take the stile beside the gate. Turn right along the lane to the T-junction with the road, where you turn left to enter Littleton Drew.

C As soon as the village road bends right, turn left down the bridleway. Follow this track around the converted barn. Continue along and up the broad green lane for about 600 metres, until you reach a T-junction in front of a field gate. Turn right, through the adjacent field gate. Initially, keep with the left-hand hedge then head across the field, past an electricity pole, to take the field gate in the far wall. Turn left along the crossing green lane, which you proceed straight along for about 1000 metres. Eventually you exit, via the gateway at the end, on to the crossing by-way. This follows the route of the old Roman road, the Fosse Way. Turn left and keep ahead. Pass West Dunley Farm, continuing along what also serves as its driveway, and through woodland, towards the main road. At the junction, keep straight ahead, still on the Fosse Way route. Just over 100 metres along the highway you reach a waymarked footpath, turning left through the hedgerow.

D Take the footpath through the gap into the field. Proceed past the electricity pole to the corner of the woodland ahead. Follow along the right-hand edge, to take the field gate into the following field. Keep straight ahead, towards further woodland visible in the distance. Then veer slightly leftwards, to take the gap in the nearer hedgerow. Cross the next field and exit via the similar gap. Keep on a similar alignment as you enter the next field. Glimpses of the spire of

Alderton church, towards which you are now heading, appear on the horizon, occasionally obscured by the tree more immediately ahead. Proceed straight ahead, through this long field, now alongside the woodland you previously observed ahead. Take the gate/stile in the hedgerow, at the far end. The following field is extensive. Continue uphill in the same direction, towards its centre. Pass about 100 metres beyond the lone tree, still on the alignment of Alderton church spire. Then bear diagonally left under the power lines and towards the field gate within the stone wall, over in the distant far left-hand corner.

E Take the stile adjacent to the field gate, to cross the wall on to the lane. Turn left, and follow the lane past farm buildings into the centre of the village of Alderton. At the duck pond, turn right on the fenced footpath alongside. Exit and turn right along the main street. Pass the village hall and follow the street around the bend towards St Margaret's church. Opposite to the church, go through the gates to take the drive to Manor Farm, passing by the pond on your left. Before the drive bears left, keep straight ahead along the waymarked path within the large adjacent field. Follow the ditch/hedgerow along the left-hand field boundary. Exit, via the field gate, on to the road, with a sewage works off to the left. Turn right up the road. Continue past the barn and the road junction. Keep with the road ahead, signed to Sherston, for about a further 200 metres to reach the crossing, waymarked path.

F Take the stile/gate off to the left, signed to Luckington Court. Follow the right-hand hedge through the field. Cross the similar stile/gate. Continue in the same direction through the next field and towards the clearly visible Luckington Court. Cross the next stile/gate. In the next field bear slightly left down the centre. At the bottom, take the further stile/gate to progress to the enclosed track. Proceed over the stream and head uphill. At the top and outside the back entrance to Luckington Court, you reach a crossing path. Go left to take the stile/gate into the churchyard of St Mary and St Ethelbert church. Follow the path through the churchyard and out to the front. Go through the gate and keep straight ahead along the fenced/walled drive, to rejoin Church Road – upon which you walked earlier. Turn right and pass the main entrance to Luckington Court. Retrace your footsteps back to the village green – with the Old Royal Ship pub nearby. **A**

No. 13

Blagdon, Ubley and Butcombe

Distance 7.25 miles / 11.5 kms

Time 3 to 3.5 hours

OS Map Explorer 141 and 154

Starting Point Car park, behind Blagdon Village Club and next to the fire station, off Station Road, Blagdon – OS reference 501592

Parking Free parking

Reaching the start from Bristol Go south on the A38. Pass Bristol Airport. Just over half-a-mile beyond the Holiday Inn, take the minor road off to the left, signed to Burrington. Turn left at the T-junction with the A368. Proceed for two miles along the A368 to reach the centre of Blagdon. Station Road is down to the left

Refreshments New Inn, Blagdon – early on the route. Suitable picnic opportunities on seats next to Blagdon Lake towards the end of the walk. Various other options in Blagdon, before or after the walk

---

THIS CIRCLE AROUND Blagdon Lake is centred around the countryside of Wrington Vale/ Chew Valley, to the south of Bristol. Much of the walk is on higher ground above the lake, affording impressive panoramic views. There is one flat section but generally the terrain is undulating. There are a few stretches that can become wet or muddy – these should always be passable but may be difficult in the winter.

The walk starts in the centre of Blagdon and soon traverses the footpath linking up with the church, with attractive vistas down towards the lake. You continue on through woodland and across farmland, via Yeo Valley Farm, to reach the village of Ubley. You proceed northwards and along the north side of the lake along a combination of footpaths and quiet country lanes to reach West Town and then Butcombe. There is then a short steep climb on to Sutton Lane, an ancient track from which there are further panoramic views. After the descent back down to the lake there is a lengthy stretch along the shore and dam. The last section comprises a steep climb via Dark Lane, another ancient track, back to the start in Blagdon.

A Exit the car park, the way you came in. Turn left down the hill for about 50 metres. Turn right into Bell Square. Take the no-through-road ahead, and soon pick up the tarmac path connecting the two sides of Blagdon and offering impressive views across Blagdon Lake and towards the tower of St Andrew's church. Follow the walled path around and downhill, via two gates. At the T-junction turn left and downhill. Continue through the gate, by the natural spring. Keep left up the path heading towards the church. Stay alongside the wall and go through another gate. Pass along and in front of the church. From the church gate, take the entrance road leading out on to Park Lane/Church Street. The New Inn is almost opposite. Turn right along Church Street. Within about 75 metres turn left along Grib Lane, from which there are more panoramic views. At the end of the lane, continue straight ahead along the walled footpath. As you descend into woodland keep straight ahead and downhill. Eventually turn left, down steps, to exit the woodland via the gate into the adjacent field. Turn right and continue down the top edge of the field. Go through the gate. In the next field continue on, as before. More than halfway along, take the small gate by an oak tree into the next field. Follow the path along the left-hand edge to exit, via the gate, on to the surfaced track. Keep ahead along the track, past the pond and through the gate, to join the crossing access road.

B Go left along the road towards the buildings of Yeo Valley Farms. After about 100 metres take the waymarked right-hand turn, through the gate and into the fenced path alongside the field. At the end take the gate, proceed over the bridge and follow the wooden railings through the tree plantation. Exit via the further gate, as waymarked. Enter the field immediately ahead and bear right towards the gate in the corner. Take successive gates to enter the following, narrow field. Veer rightwards across the field to take another gate. Bear right along the following field, to take the stile in the centre of the far hedgerow. Walk to the far-right corner of the next field, which can be muddy, to take the field gate. In the field beyond keep left along the track. Continue through the gate and past the outbuildings of Ubley Farm. As you pass the farmhouse the track morphs into Frog Lane and you enter the village of Ubley. When you reach The Street, continue straight ahead and past the village hall. About 50 metres beyond Walnut Tree Close, take the next lane off to the left: Stilemead Lane. Ahead of the recent houses at the end of the lane, turn right to take the stile into the extensive field. Bear right to pick up the right-hand field corner.

Then follow the hedgerow through the next corner, all along the field. About a further 50 metres beyond the very far corner, take the waymarked gate in the hedgerow. Head down the centre of the next field, towards the distant hillside ahead. Take the gate in the far hedgerow. Follow along the right-hand hedgerow, for about 50 metres. Take the stile/footbridge/stile, to enter the following field. Proceed to the far-left corner and exit via the gate. Follow the hedged track, to reach the road.

C Turn left along the road. You pass a prominent chimney, part of a former mill; and then the entrance to Ubley Hatchery. Continue ahead over the River Yeo. Keep left at the road junction. Just past Selways take the gate on the right, through the hedgerow and into the adjacent field. Head across the field diagonally, keeping just to the left of a telegraph pole, to take the gate/footbridge/gate. Go ahead into the next field for about 30 metres and then turn sharp right up it, in parallel with the hedgerow. Cross the further gate/footbridge/gate in the hedgerow ahead, via steps. Climb into the field beyond, in which you turn left alongside the bottom hedgerow. Take the gate into the next field and keep ahead in the same direction, with the hedgerow on your left. Go through the gate and cross the plank bridge, in the hedgerow. In the following field, bear slightly left and downhill towards the farmyard, aiming just to its right, to take the small gate. Go straight across the concrete drive of Rugmoor Farm. Continue through successive field gates, via the concrete bridge, into the adjacent field. Keep with the left-hand

hedge and through the gap, into the subsequent field. Take the gate and bridge out on to the road. Turn right and start to climb uphill. Ignore Awkward Hill off to the right, as the road bends away to the left. You pass the Coach House, before the road bends to the right up Chapel Hill.

D Almost immediately beyond the Chapel Hill road sign, go up stone steps and through the gate into the field beyond. With spectacular views of the lake and Blagdon village, climb gently and diagonally up the long field. Take the gate in the top left-hand corner and turn left along the hedged, minor road. Continue past Bellevue Farm, to reach the T-junction at Twinner's. Here, turn right and uphill. Within about 75 metres take the left-hand footpath at the entrance to Longacre Barn. Take the gate into the curtilage – and go over the stile in the hedgerow ahead, into the garden beyond. Closely follow the right-hand hedge. Pass the pond and follow the stream on your left. Exit via the gate into the adjacent field. Immediately turn right, into the next field via the stile. Go ahead, hedge right, and exit via the gate. In the next field, keep straight ahead into the following field via another gate. Continue in the same direction across marshy terrain, and through the gate beyond. You traverse another boggy area within the following field, to take the stile ahead, leading into the outer perimeter of the Brook Farm complex. Continue along the narrow field. Cross the stile, the farm drive and the further stile. Pass through the farmhouse garden and exit, via the stile, on to the road. Turn left down the road and past Mendip View Farm, to reach the edge of Butcombe.

■E Take the left-hand fork in the road and descend to the T-junction, near to the centre of the village. Turn right and uphill. Within about 75 metres take the stile in the left-hand hedge. Continue along the fenced footpath. Take another stile and follow alongside the stream. Cross the long footbridge and exit, via the next stile, into the field. Head up the field boundary towards the top left-hand corner. Turn left, to take the gate into another field. It can be muddy here, as you cross the stream again. Go forward into the field for about 50 metres and then bear right, steeply uphill. Aim initially for an electricity pole and then continue on a similar alignment, to take the gate in the hedge ahead. Turn left and continue along the crossing, hedged track – Sutton Lane – from which there are further panoramic views. Keep along the ancient track, as it contours the hillside and then curves leftwards and downhill. In the winter a small stream follows the route of the track, making a small section sometimes challenging. The track eventually broadens out into a driveway and passes several houses, as it descends to the junction with the road ahead. Cross the road, to take the stile immediately opposite into the field. Continue down the field, boundary right. In the bottom corner, take the gate into the following field. Continue downhill, now boundary left, towards the woodland on the edge of Blagdon Lake. At the corner, turn right along the woodland boundary for about 50 metres.

■F Take the gate, to enter the woodland. Ignore the footbridge straight ahead. Instead, take the path immediately off to the right, keeping within the right-hand edge of the woodland. Head

towards the edge of the lake. Cross over the next footbridge. Keep with the path, as it wends its way along the edge of the lake. There are numerous seats from which you can enjoy the views and ambience. Continue along the lakeside path and towards the obvious dam ahead. At the end exit the woodland, via the gate, and on to the road. Turn left and over the dam, towards Blagdon on the hill ahead. At the end of the dam, turn immediately left and on to Park Lane.

Proceed alongside the lake and woodland, for about 300 metres. Opposite to the entrance to Blagdon fishing lodge turn right, to take Dark Lane. Climb up this sunken and wooded track, all the way to the top. Upon exiting on to the crossing road, turn left and steeply uphill, towards Blagdon village centre. Upon returning to Bell Square, simply continue uphill for about a further 50 metres. Proceed back to the car park, from where you started. A

No. 14
Congresbury, Cleeve and Wrington

Distance 8.5 miles / 14 kms

Time 4 hours

OS Map Explorer 154

Starting Point Recreation ground car park, Gooseham Mead, off Kent Road, Congresbury. OS reference – 438639

Parking Free car park

Reaching the start from Bristol Head out of Bristol on the A370 Weston-super-Mare road. Carry on through Flax Bourton, Backwell and Cleeve to reach Congresbury. Just beyond the petrol station, turn left and downhill, to the bottom of Kent Road. The car park is off to the left, via Gooseham Mead, immediately before you reach the main junction ahead

Refreshments The Star, on the edge of Congresbury, early on the walk, after visiting Cadbury Hill; Plough Inn or Golden Lion, Wrington. Various further options in the centre of Congresbury before or after the walk

---

THIS CIRCLE explores a variety of countryside to the west Bristol. The terrain and scenery includes an ancient hill fort, extensive woodland, a pretty combe, panoramic views towards the Mendips, a historic north Somerset village and a lengthy stretch of riverside meadow.

The walk starts in the centre of Congresbury, from which you soon climb to the Iron Age fortifications of Cadbury Camp. You descend towards the extensive King's Wood, through which you continue towards the village of Cleeve. You skirt the village and enter the pretty Cleeve Wood/Goblin Combe, from which you eventually emerge on to Wrington Hill. There follows a steady descent into Wrington village. The walk concludes with a flat section alongside the River Yeo, which you follow all the way back to the start.

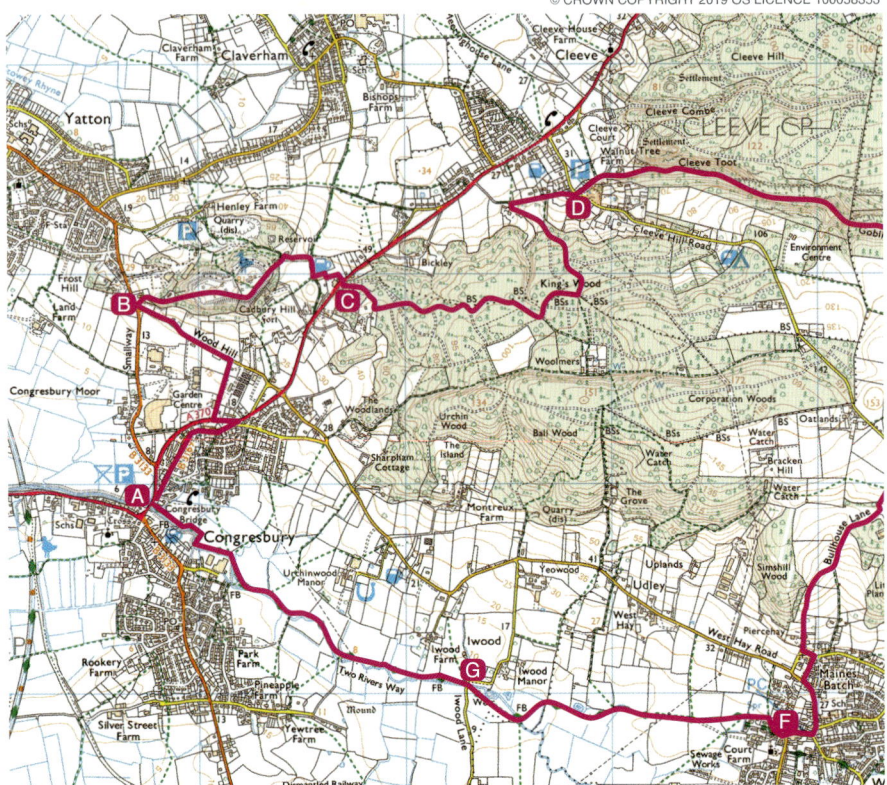

A Exit the car park via Gooseham Mead and turn right, to proceed all the way up Kent Road. When you reach the green triangle at the top, turn sharp left on the footpath to reach the main A370. Cross the road with care, and turn left along the pavement for about 30 metres. At the last of the row of houses, The Pound, take the drive and follow the left-hand hedge. Exit the grounds via the stile. Continue along the fenced/hedged footpath, passing the plant nursery and various smallholdings. Exit via the stile on to the road and turn left along it – with the wooded slopes of Cadbury Hill up on the right. Continue for about 250 metres in all, passing Westover Cottage, to reach the junction with the B3133.

B At the junction, turn right up the public footpath/track signed to Cadbury Hill. Continue up the walled track past Upper Lodge, to reach the gateway of the main house. Turn right along the path bounding the garden. Enter the curtilage of the Cadbury Hill fort and nature reserve. The fort dates back 3,000 years and is one of five Cadbury camps in the south-west of England. Follow the path uphill and as it curves around to the right. Take the gate and pass two information boards on your left, to reach the grassy plateau on top. Continue along the right-hand edge of the wooded perimeter, which is interspersed with gaps providing fine views across to the Mendips. At the first clear fork, keep right on the lesser

80

footpath – staying towards the plateau edge. Eventually this path bends back to rejoin the main track as you descend into the woodland. At the next fork, bear right alongside the wall/fence and towards the gate by further information boards. Exit on to the lane. Follow downhill past the house, Henley Wood, and around the sharp right-hand corner. Within about a 100 metres and just before farm buildings, take the gate off to the left. Follow the fenced path until exiting, via the gate, into the overgrown outer garden of the Star Inn. Exit via the further gate on to the A370. Cross the road immediately. Climb to the top of the embankment opposite, to take the small gate leading into the woodland.

C You are now in King's Wood. At the entrance there is a useful map, indicating the labyrinthine network of footpaths within. At first, proceed uphill on the footpath ahead beside the fence, then descend slightly following the wall. Stick with this same path as it bends sharp left around the corner at the cottage – beyond which you continue in a straight line. No more than 100 metres beyond the cottage, keep straight ahead over a crossing path, to soon reach a T-junction with a main surfaced track. Turn right, and follow along the track as it gently curves and climbs. Ignore several lesser side paths. At the waymarked fork keep with the left-hand track. Potentially hazardous disused mine-workings appear over to your left. At the multiple junction, keep left along the same track and continue uphill. After you negotiate the gradual right-hand bend, a tall fence appears over to the left. Continue alongside until reaching a T-junction with a major crossing path. Go left along the narrow, fenced path and over the footbridge. In front of the field gate immediately ahead, bear left and downhill. Continue as the path becomes sunken and starts to descend more steeply. Upon reaching the outer edge of the woodland, you can often see across the Severn Estuary. Exit over the stile next to the further information board. Follow the right-hand boundary down the field. As you reach the village of Cleeve take the stile near the right-hand corner. Exit on to the fenced track. Turn right and, very soon, take the gate. Turn right again along the minor road skirting the built-up edge of Cleeve. At the end, you reach a crossing road.

D Proceed straight ahead, to take Plunder Street. Take the lower driveway beyond the Goblin Combe Environmental Centre. With Walnut Farm over to your left, pass through the barrier into the Congresbury Estate and Cleeve Wood /Goblin Combe. Keep straight ahead along the track and gently up Cleeve Wood Combe, for about 1500 metres in all. Ignore all paths off to the left and right, including a prominent flight of steps. Continue until you reach the wall and information board indicating the transition into Goblin Combe. Ignore the turnings at this point also. About 400 metres further along, look out for the waymarked fork.

E Take the footpath off to the right, leading uphill through the woodland. Climb gradually up the sunken path. Eventually the path merges in with a track joining from the right, on which you keep ahead in the same direction. Exit the woodland, through the field gate by the house over to the left. Continue straight ahead on the undulating, hedged lane past Wrington Hill Farmhouse to eventually reach the T-junction ahead. Turn right along the road for about 100 metres. Turn left between farm buildings and Oaklands to take the old track: Bullhouse Lane. Keep ahead along this wooded track in the direction of Wrington. Stay with it all the way as it narrows and wends down the hillside, allowing glimpses across Wrington Vale towards the Mendip Hills. As you reach the edge of Wrington, the track morphs into a surfaced lane. After passing Long Orchard, you reach a road junction. Turn left along Roper's Lane for about 75 metres. Immediately beyond

the property, Yeomans, turn right and down the walled path. Exit via the gate at the bottom on to the driveway and then on to High Street. Turn left and follow downhill as High Street curves around to the right. Be careful, as there is no pavement. You reach the village green on the right, behind which lies the Plough Inn. At the bottom of High Street turn right into Broad Street. Take the pavement and pass in front of the Golden Lion. Keep ahead along The Triangle. All Saints' church over to your left is worth a short detour. The Triangle soon morphs into Ladywell, a residential road. Immediately before no. 9 Ladywell, take the fenced path between properties. Continue through the gate at the end. Immediately, take another gate off to the left, to enter the adjacent field.

F Upon entering the field, continue alongside the stream/fence on your left and through the gate ahead. Bear very slightly left across the following field, to take the small gate in the far hedgerow. Pass through the next field with the hedge on your right. Take the gate on the right, about 20 metres before the end. Cut across the corner of the adjacent field, to take another gate ahead. Proceed along the left-hand hedgerow of the subsequent field. About 75 metres beyond the electricity pylon, turn left through the gate in the hedgerow. Proceed along the further field to take the gate at the end. In the field beyond bear left. Stay parallel with the stream over to your right and aim for the wide bridge in the far boundary, which you cross into the following field. Continue along the field, to take the gate/footbridge/gate ahead. Bear diagonally left across the next field, towards the more significant footbridge over the River Yeo. After crossing into the field on the other side, turn right. Follow the riverbank, with Iwood Manor beyond on the opposite side. Exit via the gate on to the road. Turn right and over the bridge.

G Immediately take the footpath off to the left, via the gate. Continue in the same direction as before, but now with the river on your left. From this point onwards, you remain on this same side of the river for the remainder of the walk. Ignore several opportunities to re-cross. Follow the path along the river embankment, past the flow measuring station, through the gate and into the next field. Follow along the riverbank, through a further four fields and four gates. The tower of Congresbury church becomes apparent, a useful landmark for much

83

of the rest of the walk. In the following field, a large pipe crosses above the river. Beyond here, be sure to keep right alongside the riverbank (rather than straight ahead over the footbridge). Continue by the river, to take the gate into the next field. Keep just to the left of the power pole straight ahead and continue along the field, to take the gate beyond. Pick up the tree-lined track immediately adjacent to the river, taking you to a weir/footbridge on the edge of the built-up area of Congresbury. From the weir, take the right-hand gate into the adjacent field. Continue along the riverbank and through the next gate. Cross the narrow meadow and take the further gate ahead to enter the much larger meadow. Follow the path, as it continues along the now elevated, river embankment. Take another gate to enter the recreation area. Keep on the now surfaced path, as it continues along the still elevated embankment. Pass the modern metal bridge and advance towards the busy A370. Follow the path through the gate ahead, to re-enter the car park where you started the walk. A

No. 15

Cold Ashton, Langridge and Lansdown

Distance 10 miles / 16 kms
Time 5 to 5.5 hours
OS Map Explorer 155
Starting Point Village Hall car park, Cold Ashton – OS reference 747726
Parking Free public car park
Reaching the start from Bristol Go east on the M4. Leave by Junction 18; and then go south on the A46. At the A420 roundabout, turn left. Almost immediately, take the right-hand turn to Cold Ashton. The car park is signed, immediately off the main village street
Refreshments Blathwayt Arms, Lansdown. Also, seats with panoramic views that are ideal for picnics in the right weather conditions

---

A CHALLENGING CIRCUIT with plenty of historic interest, set at the southern tip of the Cotswold Hills – including secluded valleys and the hilltops, that form much of the Lansdown 1643 battlefield site. There are panoramic views at numerous points in the walk, most notably from Hanging Hill.

The undulating walk starts at the elevated village of Cold Ashton. It passes the historic Manor before descending into the attractive St Catherine's valley. After skirting Monkswood Reservoir and Monks Wood, the route climbs back uphill to cross the busy A46; from which it descends again to the tranquil hamlet of Langridge – where the small Norman church is worth checking out. There follows a steep climb up to Lansdown Hill; from which you proceed along the escarpment, via Bath racecourse and Lansdown Golf Club, to Hanging Hill, the main centre of the battlefield. The route follows the Cotswold Way through the battlefield site to the Grenville Monument, then gradually descends back down into a valley. The walk concludes with a steep climb through further attractive countryside, up Greenway Lane and back across the A46 to Cold Ashton and the start.

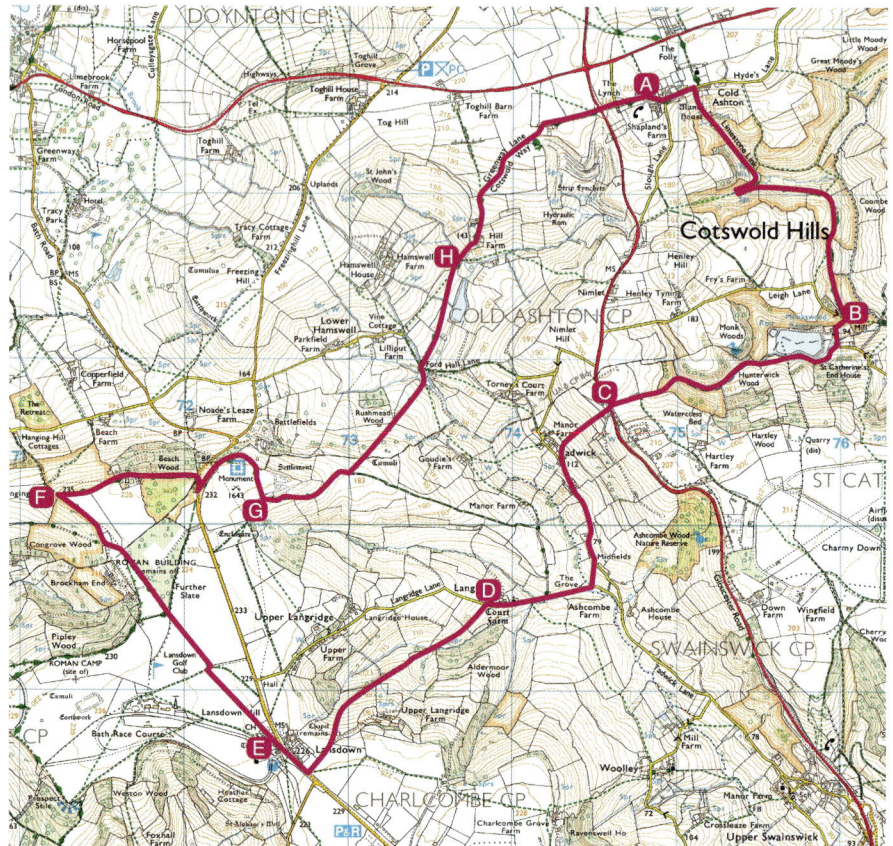

A Exit the car park and turn left, along the main village street of Cold Ashton. Continue for about 200 metres, passing the junction off to the right and the Manor. Opposite to the Old Rectory, turn right and through the gate into the field. Go straight ahead and steeply downhill, to take the gate amongst trees in the far boundary. Continue in the same direction, down to the bottom of the valley. Cross the stream to the waymark post. Follow along the far side of the stream. Conditions are often muddy, and the precise route of the path (and indeed the stream!) is not always clear. Follow the stream along the valley floor, for about 500 metres. At the end, take the gate straight ahead into the copse. Immediately turn sharp right. Follow the fence and cross the stream channel, to emerge in the adjacent field. At the waymark post turn left along the crossing path, to take the gate into the following field. Proceed generally uphill in the same direction, with the stream now down in the valley to your left. Take the obvious gate into the field up ahead. Keep close towards the left-hand boundary, along the lower path – soon passing a gate down to the left. Continue through this very large field to contour/circumnavigate the edge of the hill. Eventually take the gate leading into a sunken track. Keep ahead on the undulating track, alongside the left-hand hedge. Go through the field gate and steeply uphill, to join the crossing lane.

B Follow the lane ahead and downhill, for about 150 metres in all. You soon glimpse Monkswood Reservoir and its associated earthworks. About 50 metres after crossing the stream, turn right and through the gate into woodland. Continue ahead, up the sunken path. Pass through another gate, with the reservoir becoming gradually more visible as you gently climb. Exit the woodland, via the further gate. Go up the steps and keep ahead through the field, alongside the reservoir. Take the gate down in the right-hand corner. In the next field, keep with the right-hand boundary alongside the reservoir and then the stream. Go through the gap in the hedgerow and into the following field. Continue straight ahead up on to the plateau. No more than 75 metres into the field, deviate sharp right and downhill towards the stream. The entry point into the copse is slightly unclear, but the stile/footbridge/stile by which you cross the stream should soon become obvious. Turn left and uphill, to exit the copse. Follow the path/track with the stream on your left, for a total of about 400 metres. Ignore the field gate off to the left and keep with the level path/ track as it gently bends with the stream. When you eventually reach a small gate off to the left, go up the steps and through it. Proceed straight ahead up the steep valley side. At the top, continue through the gate and into the field ahead. Keep towards the left-hand boundary, to take the gap in the hedgerow ahead into the next field. Cross straight ahead towards the A46. Take the gate and cross the road with due care.

C On the other side of the A46, take the gate and follow the path downhill between the farm buildings and the hedgerow. Go through the paddock and take the gate into the extensive sloping field. Continue steeply down the field, keeping with the right-hand boundary. At the bottom, go through the small gate immediately ahead and take the steps down into the next field. Bear diagonally down the field, towards the hedge corner about half-way along. From here, you follow the hedgerow to take the gate down in the field corner. Descend steps on to the lane, along which you turn left. Continue along the undulating lane for about 500 metres in all, passing several properties. Just beyond Walnut Lodge look out for the path off to the right. Go through the gate, and bear diagonally left down the field towards the power pole. Continue down to the far corner. Exit via the gate at the bottom, to join another lane on the edge of the hamlet of Langridge. Turn right and up the lane, crossing the stream. Keep ahead, with the stream now over to your left. Proceed past both the right-hand junction and the footpath signed off to the left. Continue uphill to reach the 12th-century St Mary Magdalene Church – which is well worth a stop for its interesting interior and tranquil churchyard. Beyond the church, proceed uphill for about a further 100 metres, skirting the buildings of Court Farm.

87

D Immediately opposite to the main driveway to Court Farm, take the track off to the left. Go through the gate into the field and continue with the fence on your right. Take the next gate into the next field. Head diagonally towards the waymark post, down in the far right-hand corner of this large field next to the stream. Cross the stream, via the stepping stones and go through the gate. Almost immediately, turn sharp right across the bridge over the tributary stream. Climb steeply up the long field, keeping towards the right-hand boundary. At the top corner follow the track through the copse, via the field gate and into the further large field. Continue uphill on the distinct track, eventually deviating slightly left towards the prominent waymark post in the centre of the field. From the post, bear more steeply uphill towards the stile in the wall and just to the left of the prominent tree. Cross the wall and continue uphill in the same direction, to reach the waymark post, on the crossing farm drive. Turn right along the metalled drive towards the obvious main road ahead, at the top of Lansdown Hill. Exit across the cattle grid and via the gateway, on to the main road. Cross the road with care, and proceed on the verge adjacent to Bath Racecourse. Continue past the Blathwayt Arms and for about a further 50 metres beyond.

E Take the path off to the left, immediately beyond Rose Cottage. Take the gate and bear right in the direction of the golf club. Go through the car park and past the frontage of the clubhouse, towards the waymark post – from which you enter the golf course proper. Follow the clearly waymarked path running between the driving range and a line of conifers. Carry on straight ahead to cross the entrance road to the racecourse, where you reach the clearly waymarked junction of several paths. Here you proceed on the fenced/walled track straight ahead, towards distant woodland. Continue ahead in the same direction, with the golf course still on your left. Keep ahead, ignoring all

turns. Pass alongside the woodland, at the end of which you keep left with the track and the golf course boundary. Just before reaching a field gate ahead, take the railed path up to the right. Follow the path through the gate and into the spinney. Continue along this path on the top of the escarpment, with spectacular views over to the west, towards Bristol. Pass through the following gate and eventually exit the spinney into the adjacent field. Go up the field, keeping towards the left-hand boundary wall. At the corner, go past the trig point and through the gate on to Hanging Hill. You are now on the battlefield of the Battle of Lansdown: there are various information boards and signs in this vicinity and for the next part of the walk.

F From the entrance gate, keep along the top of the field with the fence/wall on your right. Pass (or pause at) the seat and proceed towards the far end. Exit through the field gate and take the enclosed path past the Fire Service complex on your right. At the end turn right along the metalled track. Within about 50 metres, take the left-hand gate to enter scrubland, within which you follow the path parallel with the access road. Exit via the small gate back on to the access road, which you follow ahead for about 100 metres – parallel with the evident main road. Look out for the footpath sign into the left-hand hedge. Go through and cross the main road. On the other side, take the gate immediately ahead. Pass the further information board and continue on the track, in the direction of the Grenville Monument – soon evident ahead. Pass the monument and descend into the woodland, keeping to the path. Cross the stepped stile over the wall. Keep ahead, following the left-hand boundary, to eventually exit the woodland up into the adjacent field. Keep along the left-hand field boundary and continue towards the stile in the corner.

G Cross the stepped stile in the wall, at which point there is more information about the Battle of Lansdown. Continue on the path down the next field, following the left-hand boundary, towards the gate in the corner. Take the field gate, and proceed down the well-hedged green lane for about 350 metres. As another field gate appears directly ahead, take the smaller gate off to the left through the hedgerow and into the adjacent field. Cross the field and take successive gates in the far right-hand corner. In the next field, head straight downhill, towards the waymark post and seat. Continue down the field, keeping to the right of the barn. Go through successive gates into the next field. Continue straight down the slope, homing in on the cattle grid on the crossing lane below. On reaching the lane turn left and across the stream and cattle grid. Continue uphill for about 100 metres, via another cattle grid. Immediately beyond Brook Cottage, take the track off to the right. Go through the gate to enter the following field. Identify the prominent Hill Farm in the distance – a useful landmark in navigating the next few fields. Bear slightly left across the first field, to exit via the gateway in the far hedgerow. In the next field, keep ahead in the same direction, with a lake evident over to your right. Go through another gateway. In the following field, keep ahead towards the left-hand edge of the woodland, still on the alignment of Hill Farm. Pass the corner of the woodland and continue alongside it towards the field corner ahead, avoiding the boggy area as best you can. Take the gate into the woodland, cross the stream and exit on to the crossing track – Greenways Lane – which you now follow for most of the way back to Cold Ashton.

H Climb steeply up the lane, passing Hill Farm on your right. The gradient gradually eases – but you continue uphill on the lane, for about 1000 metres in all. On route you pass by Special Plants, Little Ballthorns Farm and Greenways Farm. Cold Ashton becomes increasingly obvious ahead. Cross the main A46 and continue steeply up the road immediately opposite. At the top you join the main village street, which you continue along for just over 100 metres. The village hall car park, where you started, is off to the left. **A**

No. 16
Box and Box Hill

Distance 8 miles / 13 kms
Time 3.5 to 4 hours
OS Map Explorer 156
Starting Point Selwyn Hall car park, Valens Terrace, off the High Street, Box – OS reference 823686
Parking Free parking, Selwyn Hall car park
Reaching the start from Bristol Go east on the M4. Leave by Junction 18 and then go south on the A46. At Batheaston, pick up the A4 and proceed eastwards for a further three miles to Box. Once in Box, bear left to stay with the A4. Very soon after the traffic lights, and just beyond the Bengal Bear restaurant, look out for the sign off to the left
Refreshments Quarryman's Arms, Box Hill; plus various options in Box

---

THIS WALK explores the countryside near to Bath on the south-eastern fringes of the Cotswold Hills. It encompasses the linked villages of Box and Box Hill, a long stretch of riverbank, various pockets of woodland, Hazelbury Manor and extensive panoramic views. The terrain is mainly flat but there are several short climbs. Parts of the riverside section can be muddy

The route starts in the centre of Box. The first third of the walk progresses alongside the Bybrook river, through meadows, fields and woodland. After crossing the river, you climb through further woodland to reach the edge of Rudloe, before continuing further back along the valley towards Box Hill village. The walk climbs through the village and back into open countryside, to reach Hazelbury Manor. There follows a circuitous and undulating walk through combes/woodland. You eventually ascend to Blue Vein, from which there are extensive panoramic views towards Box and Colerne. There follows a, mainly, gradual descent back to Box via fields, woodland and the interesting hamlet of Washwell.

A From the Selwyn Hall car park, enter the large recreation ground via the path up the slope, by the telegraph pole. Proceed along the embankment, bisecting the cricket and football grounds. At the end turn left towards the corner. Aim for the small bridge in the wooded area, about 30 metres to the left of the corner. Cross the stream, turn right and proceed along the fenced path. Exit via the gate on to the road. Turn left under the railway bridge and continue over the first of successive bridges.

B Before the second bridge take the footpath down to the right by the Bybrook river – which you now follow along for about 3000 metres in all. Proceed along the wooded riverbank. Follow the path across the river via successive footbridges. Continue along the fenced boundary. Exit the woodland via the gate into the adjacent meadow. Carry on ahead, keeping the river to your right. You reach the power-line and continue parallel with it. After passing through the next gate and under the power-line, keep by the river. After about a further 300 metres, veer slightly left and uphill to take the gate in the hedgerow ahead. In the next field keep with the right-hand hedgerow. Exit, via the gate, on to the lane. Turn right and downhill. At the junction turn left towards Saltbox Farm. Immediately past the farm, take the stile straight ahead into the field beyond. Head slightly left, across the field. Follow along the modest ditch/embankment, then bear towards the small gate in the boundary ahead, near to the river. Within the next, extensive field, simply keep alongside the river and approach the farm buildings ahead. At the far boundary take the small gate to reach the lane. Follow the lane straight ahead, passing the Widdenham Farm complex. Proceed to the end of the lane. Ignore the crossing bridleway to continue, through the field gate, into the further meadow. Keep straight ahead through the meadow – contouring the hillside with the river down to your right. Keep ahead to take the small gate into the next meadow. Carry on in the same direction, on the fringe of woodland. Take the small gate leading on to the fenced path, following the outer perimeter of Colerne Park/Monks Wood – managed by the Woodland Trust. Advance along the path until it eventually enters the woodland at a merging of paths. Turn right, to continue in the same direction. Exit the woodland and cross the bridge, over the river. Continue along the fenced path, as it curves right and away from the woodland. Exit, via the gate, on to the following track.

C Immediately beyond the gate cross the tributary stream. Proceed up the fenced track, which soon bends away to the right. Continue, increasingly steeply uphill, to take the field gate. Enter the woodland ahead and continue uphill through it, ignoring all turns. You emerge from the woodland to enjoy fine views of Colerne church and the valley beneath. Continue up the now bounded track and through the gate, to reach the pair of cottages ahead. Follow the now tarmacked lane straight ahead and as it curves around to the left, past Bybrook View, the redevelopment of the former RAF establishment, Rudloe Manor. Upon reaching the main entrance to Bybrook View, keep ahead along the lane for about a further 250 metres. Take the

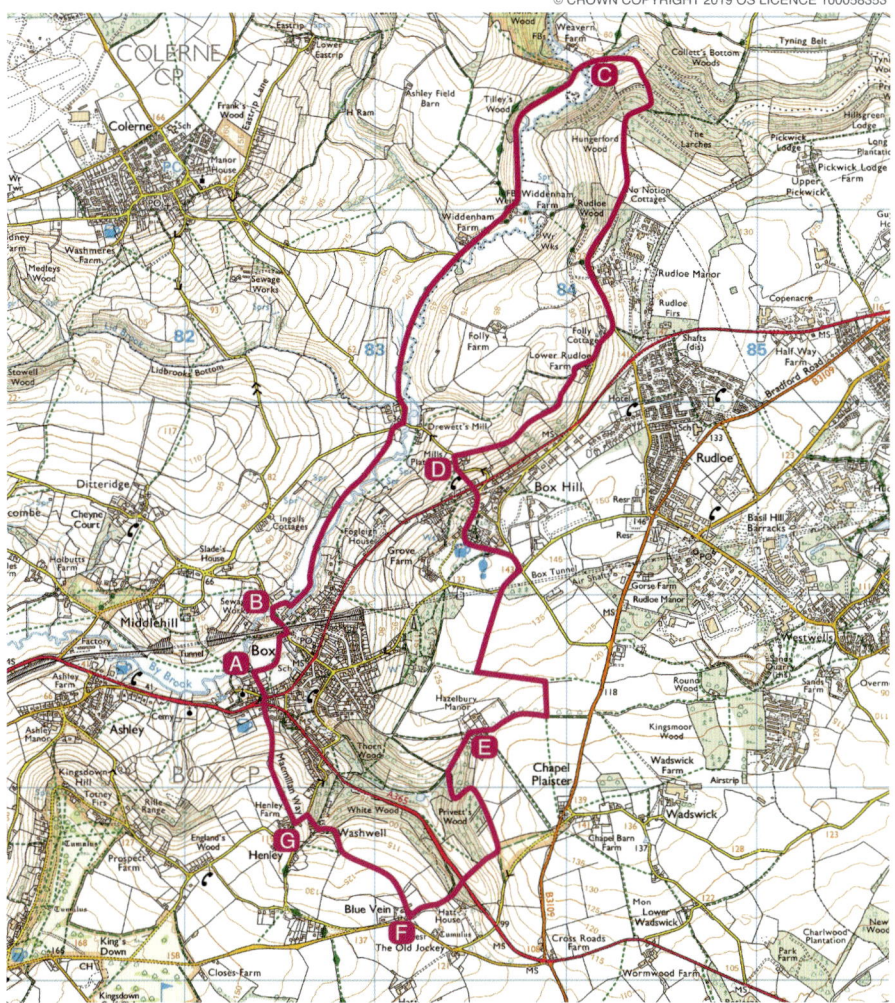

right-hand turn and proceed downhill. Pass Folly Cottage on your right. Immediately before the farm ahead, indicated as offering bed and breakfast accommodation, take the footpath off to the right, running along its outer perimeter. Continue along this fenced and tree-lined footpath for about a further 800 metres in all, contouring the hillside along the valley. The path runs in parallel with the route of the A4 main road, audible but not intrusive, up to your left. Take the metal gate, to go through the copse adjacent to a field. Continue into the field, and keep along its top boundary, to reach the gate in the corner. Exit via the gate down to the lane ahead. Turn left and climb uphill. Within no more than 50 metres – and just as the lane swings around to the left – take the steps ahead.

D Climb the waymarked stile into the paddock. Walk uphill, boundary right. Exit via the stile, to cross the A4 with care. On the other side, proceed up the steps and the path between the houses, to reach the junction. Continue straight ahead up Barnetts Hill. At the next junction bear right towards the Quarrymans Arms public house. Just past the front entrance to the pub, bear left and up the signed footpath/lane. Pass the pillar box and bend around to the left, in front of several cottages. Immediately beyond Tisbutts Cottage the lane morphs into a path and ascends through woodland. Down on the left there are tennis courts, located in what was once a deep quarry. Keep along the narrow, fenced path, which soon emerges from the woodland. Pass through two stone stiles, to reach the road. Turn right and walk to the crossroads. Turn right again and continue for about a further 75 metres. As the road bends away to the right, proceed straight ahead via the gate into the field beyond. Initially follow the right-hand boundary and, as the field opens out, keep ahead on the same alignment towards the complex of buildings beyond – Hazelbury Manor. At the far side, turn left and proceed with the wall on your right. Follow this for about 300 metres until reaching an obvious gap, through which you turn right. Go straight across the next field on the well-defined path, exiting via the gap in the row of trees on the far side. Turn right along the driveway leading to Hazelbury Manor. Pass the green barn and go through the outer gardens to approach the manor. On reaching the junction with the main driveway in front of the house, turn right. Proceed for a short distance, facing the house, before turning left. Pass the pond and group of agricultural outbuildings.

E Immediately beyond the outbuildings, turn left down the fenced/walled track, into woodland. Continue down the track until reaching the field gate straight ahead. Do not take this; instead bend left and over the bridge – where it is usually muddy. Keep uphill with the track as it bends left and right. When you emerge from the woodland on to the open plateau, be careful: do not continue any further on the track ahead. Instead, turn sharp right alongside the right-hand hedgerow. Within about 50 metres, take the concealed stile into the adjacent field. Proceed downhill, keeping to the right-hand boundary. After descending steeply to the bottom, climb back up the field. Take the steps and the stile in the right-hand corner, to reach the A365. Cross the main road and take the waymarked footpath, almost immediately opposite, into the woodland. Proceed up the well-marked footpath. After about 50 metres, you reach a handrailed section. Beyond this, turn left along the crossing, sunken track. Continue uphill, towards the high wall – and follow this along, as it curves around to the right. After passing the new Cotswold stone house, proceed past the outbuildings of Blue Vein Farm. Exit the woodland to join the driveway to the main farmhouse.

F Turn right along the driveway. Almost immediately take the small gate into the garden. Follow the clear waymarks through the garden, via two stiles, into the extensive field ahead. Descend most of the length of the field, on a line just to the left of the prominent water-tower on the distant horizon. As you come within less than 50 metres of the bottom hedgerow, keep left and downhill, towards the far field corner. Look out for the small wooden stile, which is not easily visible until you are near it. Cross the stile into woodland. Descend straight

ahead and steeply, in the direction of the dwellings visible below. As you emerge from the woodland at the bottom of the slope, fork right at the junction of paths. The path climbs back uphill and morphs into a tarmac path. Continue uphill, past the cottages on your left, to reach the road ahead. Turn left and follow the road uphill for about 100 metres, until you encounter further houses ahead.

G Just before the first house on the right, climb the steps to take the stile in the wall. You now follow the fenced/walled path downhill. Box becomes increasingly visible below, as you descend towards it. Go through the gate and keep straight ahead, down the hedged track. Pass through the market garden, keeping to the right of the greenhouses. Proceed through the next gate and then stick with the left-hand boundary. The now narrow path descends, between buildings, to the road. Cross over the A365 again, and then follow the ginnel down to the High Street. (You can detour by turning right along the High Street for about 500 metres to the railway bridge, to view at close quarters the west portal of the famous Box tunnel, engineered by Isambard Kingdom Brunel and completed in 1841.) To conclude the walk – cross the High Street, turn right and, almost immediately, left. Descend Valens Terrace to reach the Selwyn Hall car park, where you started. **A**

No. 17
Sherston and Easton Grey

Distance 7.5 miles / 12 kms
Time 3 to 3.5 hours
OS Map Explorer 168
Starting Point Post Office Stores, High Street, Sherston – OS reference 853859
Parking Plenty of free parking in High Street, Sherston
Reaching the start from Bristol Go east on the M4. Leave by Junction 18 and then go north on the A46. At the traffic lights at Old Sodbury, turn right to take the B4040 Malmesbury road. Continue on through Acton Turville and Luckington. Follow the signs through to Sherston
Refreshments Rattlebones Inn; plus various other options in Sherston

---

AN EASY, ALMOST LEVEL, south Cotswolds walk along quiet lanes and field paths – including the attractive villages of Sherston and Easton Grey and a long stretch of the ancient Fosse Way. Much of the walk runs near to the River Avon, which you cross on several occasions.

The walk starts in the centre of the village of Sherston. You exit the village eastwards, to go through Pinkney Park, past Easton Grey House and through Easton Grey village. From here, the route takes you across fields and scrubland to reach the Roman Fosse Way. There follows a long section along the original Fosse Way route. The walk eventually deviates back towards Sherston across fields and through the grounds of Lordswood House. The final section of the walk is along Commonwood Lane, and then downhill through informal parkland to cross the river for the last time and return to the centre of Sherston.

🅰 From the Post Office, go north-east along the High Street and towards the church. Immediately beyond the Rattlebones Inn turn right down Noble Street. Where Grove Road forks off to the right, keep left and downhill. Within about a further 50 metres, climb the steps leading up to the left. Cross the estate road and keep ahead on the enclosed footpath. Go through the gate and follow the now wider and tree-lined path along the edge of the built-up area. Take the gate at the end into the field ahead. Bear gently right across the field, to climb the stile in the wooden fence ahead. In the next field pass to the right of the stone barn, to take the gate and exit down steps. Turn right, down the road to cross the bridge over the River Avon – the first of several crossings during the walk.

Immediately beyond the bridge, take the road leading off to the left. Proceed uphill through/alongside woodland, for about 300 metres. At the far edge of the woodland you reach the gates into Pinkney Park.

🅱 Turn left through the gates and follow the track through the parkland, staying with the left-hand boundary. Leave the parkland via the tall gate, into the adjacent field. Keep alongside the boundary wall as it bends around to the left. Exit via the field gate. Immediately turn right and then left to take the small gate into the paddock. Follow the right-hand fence/hedgerow to the corner where you continue sharp left, still following the boundary. With Park Farm over to your left, cross successive stiles into the adja-

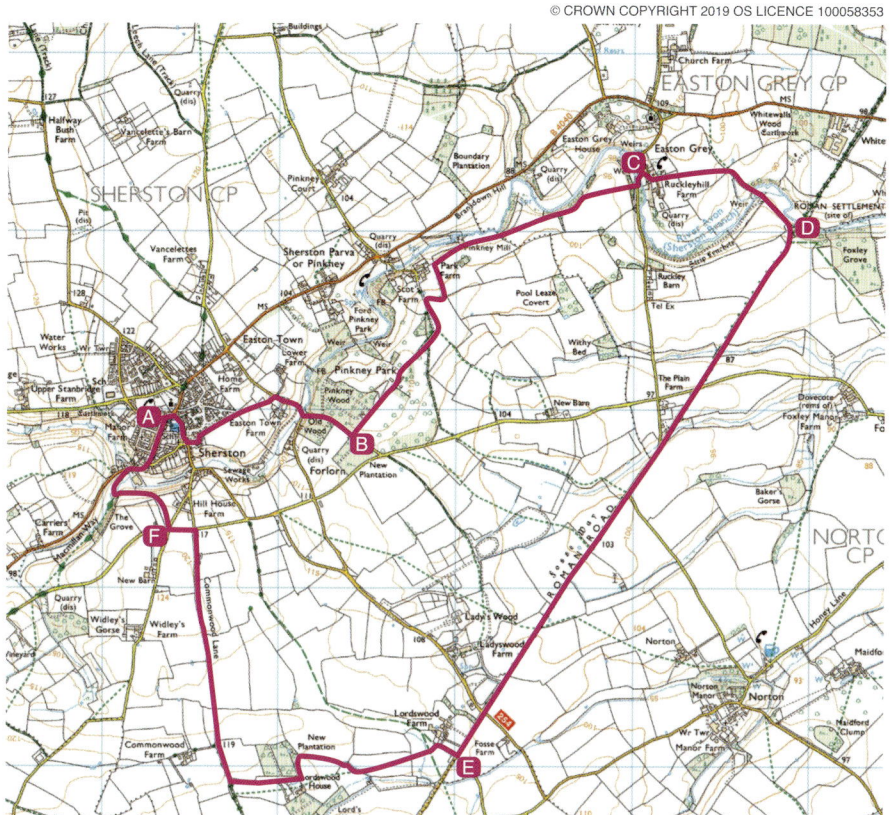

cent field. Pick up the left-hand boundary, aiming for the stile in the left-hand corner. Take the stile and continue up the long field, with the hedgerow on your left. Take the next stile, at the top of the field, to enter scrubland. Immediately curve to the right and uphill for about 30 metres, to take the gate in the fence into the extensive field beyond. Turn left, keeping alongside the fence for almost 100 metres. Keep on the higher plateau and bear towards the far boundary, aiming for the gateway gap, situated between the woodland and the left-hand corner of the field ahead. As you proceed views open up of Easton Grey House. Through the gap, follow the short, fenced track. At the end take the stile into the spinney. Cross the footbridge and exit via the following stile. In the long field ahead, proceed past the pheasant enclosures. Keep alongside the left-hand boundary as closer views open up of Easton Grey House – once the retreat of former Prime Minister Herbert Asquith. At the end of the field follow the track downhill, to take the gate out on to the road.

C Turn left along the road and across the bridge over the River Avon, to enter the village of Easton Grey. Immediately beyond the bridge, turn right and follow the minor road uphill. At the top bear

left and follow the footpath along the driveway and into the stable-yard. Take the field gate ahead. Continue straight up the field, to take the stile in the fence about 50 metres from the left-hand corner. Continue in the same direction, diagonally across the following field. Aim for the wide gap in the far boundary, near to the right-hand corner. Through the gap turn right, along the boundary hedge of the following field. At the corner, continue straight ahead directly into the scrubland. Follow the footpath downhill, alongside the wall. Cross the River Avon again, via the footbridge. This can be a suitable spot for a picnic stop. Proceed past derelict mill buildings and through two field gates in close succession. Keep ahead on the short, hedged track to emerge in the following field. Walk along the left-hand edge. Exit via the gate in the corner. Descend the wooded, sunken track towards the river-bank once again. Take the gate at the bottom, to join the route of the crossing Fosse Way. From this junction onwards, you will be tracking over 3000 metres of the original route of this Roman road.

D From the junction turn right and climb the fenced Fosse Way track. Although the climb is briefly steep, the terrain soon levels out. After going through the barrier/gate, keeping out motor vehicles – simply continue ahead on the tree-lined track for about 1000 metres. Pass through another barrier/gate. Go over the crossing road that soon follows. Keep ahead on the similar track for about a further 300 metres. Upon reaching the next road, turn left and follow it gently uphill for about 200 metres. As the road bends away to the left, go straight ahead along the broad, surfaced byway. Continue for about a further 1300 metres. When you arrive at a crossroads, keep straight ahead on the road signed for Grittleton, still on the alignment of the Fosse Way. Proceed along the right-hand verge past Lordswood Farm and for about a further 200 metres in all.

E Immediately beyond Lordswood Farm turn right, via the gate, to take the track leading into the adjacent field. Keep along the right-hand boundary, until reaching the far boundary wall corner of the farmhouse garden. Bear left in the general direction of Lordswood House, which should be visible in the far distance. Go just to the right of a power pole, to pick up the track bridging the ditch immediately ahead. Keep left, to take the gateway in the boundary ahead leading through into the next field. Go straight along this field, still in the direction of Lordswood House (although, you may need to detour around the left-hand boundary when the field is planted). Take the similar gateway in the hedgerow, at the far end. In the next field, follow the right-hand boundary all the way along the hedgerow and around the edge of the woodland. Take the stile in the far right-hand corner, to enter the grounds of Lordswood House. Keep towards the right-hand boundary, passing the pond and seat. Continue through the metal gate and keep ahead, in parallel with the driveway, and with the cricket ground over on the other side. Exit via the gate in the far right-hand corner, on to the lane ahead.

F Turn right along Commonwood Lane, which you follow for about 1400 metres in all. You pass Commonwood Farm and the Stables, a smallholding. You eventually arrive at a crossroads with the built-up area of Sherston obvious ahead. Turn left and, within about 100 metres, reach another crossroads. Go over and take the stile immediately on the right, to enter the adjacent field. Follow the left-hand hedgerow down to the field end. Bear left, through the gap in the corner and into the next field. Descend diagonally all the way down, to take the gate in the furthest right-hand corner. Immediately bend sharp left and descend towards the footbridge. Join the crossing footpath and take the footbridge over the River Avon. Turn right alongside the river and through the meadow. On reaching the meadow end, bear sharp left to take the stile/gate in the far corner, leading out on to the main road. Turn right and up the road. Be careful, as there is no pavement for much of the way up Brook Hill, which soon merges into Sherston High Street, from where you started the walk.
A

No. 18
Kellaways, Bremhill and East Tytherton

Distance 8.5 miles / 14 kms
Time 4 hours
OS Map Explorer 156
Starting Point Kellaways Bridge, Kellaways – OS reference 947757
Parking Free parking on the roadside, by or near to Kellaways Bridge
Reaching the start from Bristol Go east on the M4. Leave by Junction 17. Take the B4122, signed to Sutton Benger, to its junction with the B4069. Turn right and proceed for two miles, via Kington Langley. Turn left to Langley Burrell (easily missed). Proceed through Langley Burrell and under the railway bridge. Upon reaching the sporadic settlement of Kellaways, look out for the river bridge. The parking is mainly immediately beyond
Refreshments Dumb Post Inn, near Bremhill

MUCH OF THE WALK is along country tracks and roads, including a part of Maud Heath's Causeway. Maud Heath died in 1474, bequeathing her life savings for this route to be constructed and maintained from Wick Hill to Chippenham, a distance of about 4.5 miles. The walk is generally flat, with a couple of stretches along rivers and a single sustained climb. The meadows can be wet and/or overgrown. The extent of nettles, thistles and brambles here compel the wearing of long trousers, unless you prefer the easier alternative route.

The walk starts on the causeway at Kellaways Bridge. It passes, through the meadows of the River Avon, to the hamlet of Tytherton Lucas and continues, via fields and along a disused railway line, to pick up the tributary River Marden. At Stanley Bridge you take the road and climb steeply uphill, until diverting through woodland to Dumb Post Hill. The route continues to Bremhill village and on through farmland to reach the start of the causeway, at the top of Wick Hill. You divert along and down the escarpment, enjoying panoramic views, to reach East Tytherton – from where you follow the path of the causeway alongside the road, all the way back to Kellaways Bridge.

A Start towards the western end of Kellaways Bridge – opposite to the monument to Maud Heath. Take the stone steps down into the meadow. Proceed along the edge of the River Avon. Cross the bridge over the ditch, into the next meadow and keep alongside the river. Go through the neck of land into the next meadow. Continue next to the river until you reach the gated footbridge, which you cross to enter the meadow on the other side. Keep ahead for almost 300 metres, along the tree-lined boundary/tributary stream.

B Turn sharp left to follow the dispersed line of trees, across the meadow and towards the further footbridge. Take the gate and cross the bridge. Keep straight ahead through the field, to pick up the farm track ahead. Continue through the field gate and past Stokes and Manor Farm, to reach the road junction at the hamlet of Tytherton Lucas. Turn right for about 50 metres. Just beyond the footpath entrance to St Nicholas church, go through the farm gates into the adjacent field. Follow along the right-hand field boundary, keep straight ahead over the ditch and into the next field. Continue along the left-hand boundary hedge, to the bottom corner. Turn right with the hedgerow and alongside the river. In just over 100 metres, take the footbridge to cross over the river. On the other side, take the gate and proceed straight across the narrow field. Take the stile into the extensive field ahead. Go up the field, perhaps through crops, aiming towards the electricity pole on the rise. Keep on a straight alignment, to take the stile in the far hedgerow, with New Leaze farmhouse about 50 metres over to your right.

In the next field continue straight ahead towards the metal gates, with the built-up area of Chippenham evident in the distance beyond. Pick up the metalled farm drive and then cross the cattle grid, to reach the gates.

C At the gates turn left along the fenced track – a disused railway and now the Calne–Chippenham cycleway. Continue, for about 600 metres, until the junction with a crossing track joining from the right.

D At this point, if you prefer not to risk the wild vegetation along the riverbank, you can simply continue straight-ahead on the former railway line, take the gate on to the road ahead, turn left along the road and rejoin the walk at **E**. To proceed on the preferred route: take the field gate into the field off to the left. Climb the grassy track, to take the gateway through the hedgerow at the top. Continue down the next field, in the same direction. Pass the electricity pole, about 75 metres beyond which you take the field gate into scrubland. Proceed straight ahead on the path, through the gap and over the tributary stream into the wild meadow. Continue through the motley wild vegetation, on the sometimes barely discernible path. The odd diversion may prove necessary – the key principle being to stick near to the River Marden, on your left. You eventually take the stile next to the river, in the far corner of the meadow. Continue along the fenced path on the riverbank and beside successive fields, crossing another stile on route. Continue past the water measuring station to eventually exit, via the next stile, on to the road.

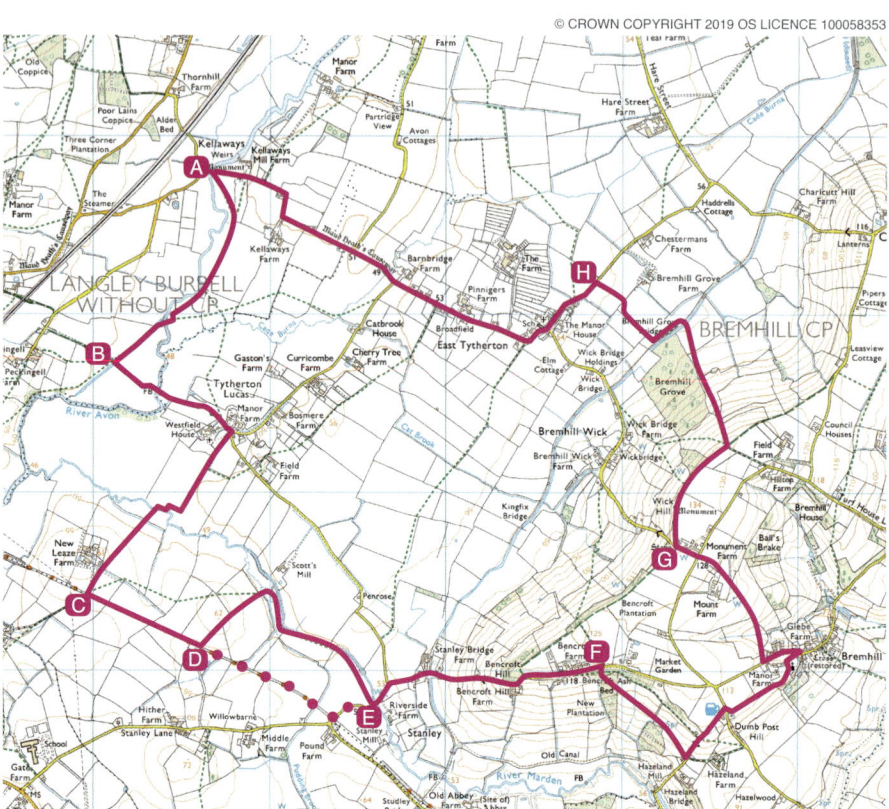

E Turn left along the road and over the river bridge; the road is narrow in places so care is required. Pass Riverside Farm and the disused chapel on your right, beyond which you start to climb significantly. After you pass Stanley Bridge Farm, the road steeply climbs Bencroft Hill. Towards the top the road bends left and right and then levels out. Pass the extensive Bencroft Farm complex on your left (ignoring the footpath running across the garden opposite). Continue ahead until you reach the waymarked, crossing path leading into the woodland on your right.

F Turn right to take the woodland path. Pass through the gate and keep on down through the woodland. Exit, via the gate in the field corner into the adjacent field. Initially follow the right-hand boundary and continue through the field in the same direction – crossing the minor stream and aiming for the field gate ahead. Take the stile next to the gate. In the following field, immediately take the lesser, left-hand fork. Head up the left-hand slope, to take the gate into the woodland. Immediately turn right along the crossing footpath. Proceed through an extensive garden area, including vari-

ous outbuildings. Eventually pass Thimble Hall to emerge, via the driveway, on to the lane ahead. Turn left up the lane, climbing the hill towards the road junction, with the Dumb Post Inn on your right. Before the actual junction, head straight down the grass slope in front of the pub, towards the footpath sign opposite. Take the driveway beside the thatched cottage and its associated garage. Pass through the squeezer stile and into the following field. Walk along the top of the field – over to the right you can see the Lansdowne Monument and the White Horse on Cherhill Down. Continue through the small gate and along the top of the next field. Take the further small gate and continue on the fenced path, through various garden areas into Bremhill village with St Martin's church ahead. Enter the church-yard and keep left. Follow the path alongside the left-hand wall, to take the gate accessing the main village street. (The stepped medieval cross in front of the church is worth a short detour.) The route continues left. Cross the village street and pass the row of cottages, Lodowicks, and then a series of further dwellings. At the edge of the built-up area, just before the speed limit signs, turn right to take the track. After about 40 metres, climb the stile by the field gate to enter the following field. Head slightly right and downhill, towards the lower ground, to cross the brook. Climb back towards the top of the field. Take the small gate into the next field, which is full of recently planted trees. Keep uphill, alongside the left-hand hedge. At the top of the field climb the stile. From here keep straight ahead along the fenced

track, continuing as it merges with the driveway. Exit the driveway on to the road, opposite to Monument Farm. Immediately cross and continue straight ahead on the joining road, alongside Monument Farm and towards the row of pine trees. Just as the road begins to descend, stop to read the inscribed stone in the hedgerow on the left, marking the start of Maud Heath's Causeway.

G Immediately opposite to the inscription, cross the stile. Walk along the field to the (further) Lansdowne Monument, erected in 1838. Past the monument, keep to the left-hand boundary and head for the field gate. Go through and into the next field. Keep ahead in the same direction, adjacent to the hedge/woodland. Take the small gate into the next field, where panoramic views soon open up to your left. At the field end, turn sharp left to take the double-gates in the left-hand corner. Head down the escarpment on the clear track. Take more double-gates into the next field. Continue down the track, with woodland on your left. Go through the next field gate and into the following field. Keep adjacent to the woodland and head towards the bottom corner. Turn right along the boundary, for about 50 metres, until reaching the path leading through the hedge. Cross the footbridge and, with the imposing Bremhill Grove Farm ahead, take the gate into the next field. Immediately, turn left and keep alongside the hedgerow. Turn right at the corner and keep alongside the recently planted trees. Go through the right-hand gap in the hedgerow ahead. In the next field, initially, keep with the left-hand boundary before cutting across the far corner and through the gap in the hedgerow beyond. Follow the fenced/hedged track, to take the gate at the end, through the hedgerow and on to the road ahead.

H Turn left along the road and continue to the village of East Tytherton. After passing the village hall, you arrive at the village green. At the road junction just beyond, go straight ahead on the Bremhill – Kellaways road (here signed only to Langley Burrell). This reconnects you with the route of the Maud Heath's Causeway, which you now track, for about 2000 metres in all. The pavement/causeway starts along the right-hand side of the carriageway. It soon switches over to the left-hand side at Forge Cottage – in due course switching back over to the right-hand side beyond Ivy Cottage. Throughout there are only intermittent signs of the original causeway. You pass various cottages and farms, to reach the eastern edge of the dispersed hamlet of Kellaways. As you pass Kellaways Farm, the pavement/causeway switches back again to the left-hand side of the road. You pass Kellaway Mills Farm and St Giles church, before the raised section of causeway reappears beyond. The end of the walk is now in sight. **A**

No. 19
Nailsworth, Kingscote and Horsley

Distance 9 miles / 14.5 kms

Time 4.5 hours

OS Map Explorer 168

Starting Point Cossack Square, at the junction of Old Market, Newmarket Road and Chestnut Hill, in the centre of Nailsworth – OS reference 848995

Parking Free long-stay public car park beyond the Britannia Inn, off Newmarket Road, Nailsworth. Other similar options available near to the starting point

Reaching the start from Bristol Go east on the M4. Leave by Junction 18 and then go north on the A46. Carry on all the way to the roundabout, in the centre of Nailsworth. Here turn left and immediately left again, to reach Old Market. Pass the Bus Station to reach the junction from which the walk starts, and the car park beyond

Refreshments The Hog, Horsley; Britannia Inn and plenty of other options in Nailsworth

---

AN UNDULATING WALK starting in the Cotswold wool town of Nailsworth and exploring the attractive woodlands, valleys and countryside to the south of Stroud. The route passes through the tranquil village of Kingscote and a secluded valley with millponds, near to the end. In the main it follows well-trodden tracks and footpaths, but a few sections become overgrown in the summer months.

The walk proceeds steeply out of Nailsworth up Chestnut Hill and westwards through woodland along Buntings Hill, before dropping down into Miry Brook valley. There follows an ascent to Lower Lutheredge Farm, from where you continue on up a well-defined track to Upper Lutheredge Farm. The route diverts across fields, over the B4058 and through Woodleaze Farm. You pass through Kingscote Wood for the first time and then uphill to Kingscote village. The route proceeds northwards, across fields and via a further extensive area of Kingscote Wood; climbing to exit at the village of Horsley. There follows a steep descent into the valley below. The valley takes you to Housley Mill and alongside mill ponds towards Ruskin Mill. In the final section you weave your way, uphill and downhill, along various urban footpaths to return to the start, in Nailsworth town centre.

A From Cossack Square, off Old Market and opposite to the Britannia Inn, climb Chestnut Hill. The road is signed to the Quaker Meeting House, which you soon pass, as you climb steeply to the T-junction, with The Roller. Turn right and almost immediately left, into the at first narrow, Dark Lane. Continue uphill for a total of about 500 metres as the lane widens and narrows again, until reaching a crossroads. Turn left on the clearly indicated Seven Acres Road and descend steeply for about 100 metres. As the road curves around to the right, divert up the hedged footpath. This soon leads you up into woodland, undulating around the edge of Buntings Hill betwixt parcels of housing. Keep along the path for about 300 metres, until reaching a very definite cross-path junction with a waymark post at its centre.

B Turn right and uphill. After another waymark post, the path curves around to the left and heads steeply uphill. Continue to the top of the slope, to reach the junction with a crossing path/track immediately in front of metal field gates (the Forest Green Rovers football ground is over to the right). Turn sharp left and follow the path/track downhill, adjacent to the embankment. Keep along this path/track, as it descends and meanders. (Ignore the downhill turning off to the left.) Continue along the path/track, as it bends around to the right, briefly narrows and then climbs steadily again. Proceed until you reach the junction of paths at an opening under power lines. Turn sharp left on to the path following the power lines downhill. After only about 30 metres, take the further sharp left turn on to the lesser path. Complete a hair-pin bend, back under the power lines, to re-enter the woodland. Proceed downhill; the first 50 metres or so of the path will be overgrown. A more major path merges from the right. Carry on down the valley side (this can be overgrown but it should always be passable with persistence and care). As you approach the valley floor, turn sharp right along the waymarked path and follow it along the stream. Within about 100 metres take the fork down to the left, to cross the footbridge. Climb the stile and continue up through the scrubby fringes of the woodland. After about 75 metres, take the further stile, to exit the woodland into the adjacent field. Head steeply up the field, alongside the left-hand hedge until joining the crossing track in the corner. Follow the track further uphill, to the top of field. Take the field gate, to join the crossing farm track.

C Turn right and follow the metalled track gently upwards and past Lower Lutheredge Farm. Go through the field gate and keep up the track as it becomes fenced. Take successive field gates, to pass barns. Proceed gradually through the next field and field gate. Continue along the right-hand hedgerow of the following field and through the further field gate. Keep ahead on the now enclosed track, pass Upper Lutheredge Farm – down to your right – and take the following gate, to join the driveway. Turn left and, almost immediately, exit the driveway for the following lane. Keep ahead for about 75 metres, beyond a (slightly confusing) footpath sign on your left.

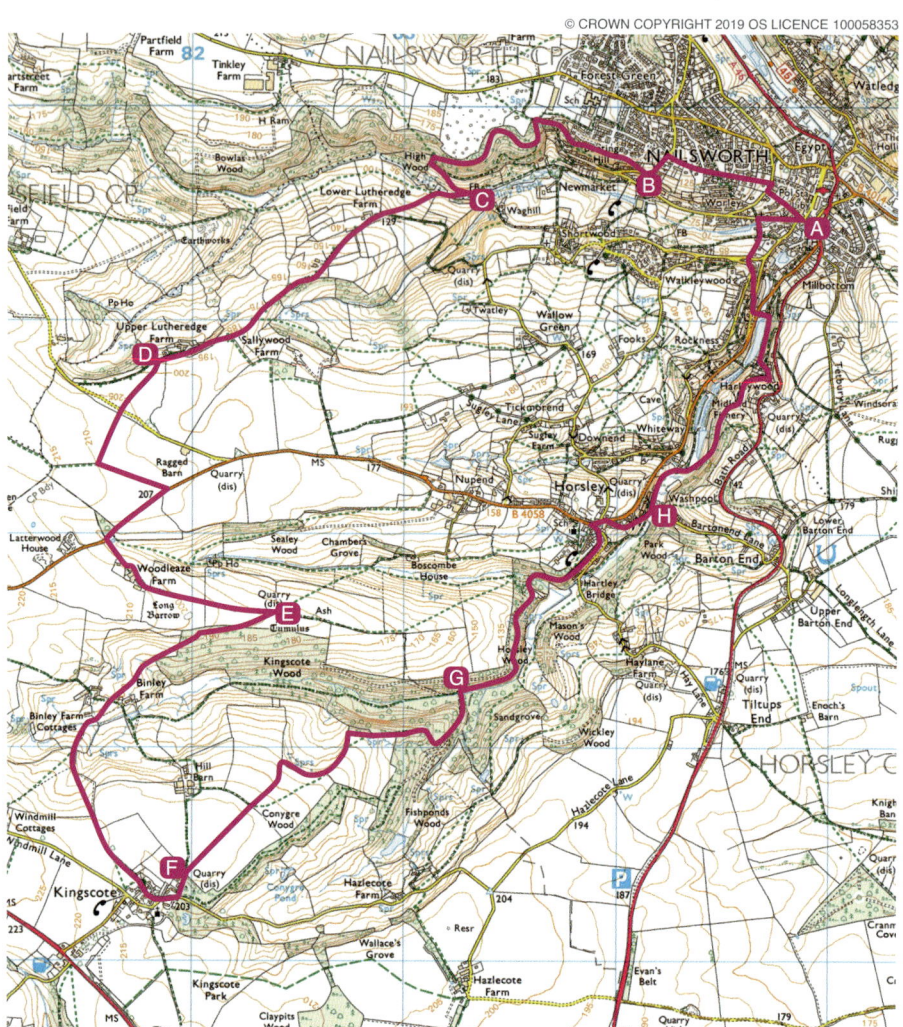

🅓 Take the field gate into the extensive field. Bear right and uphill – heading in the direction of the stile in front of the lone tree in the far hedgerow. Take the stile, cross the lane and then two further stiles in short succession. Enter the field and aim straight ahead for the (usually) obvious gap in the hedgerow ahead. If the field is cropped, you may have to divert all the way around the field boundary. Beyond the gap, turn immediately left in the following field and keep alongside the boundary, all the way to the corner. Take the field gate in the far boundary, to exit out on to the main road. Turn right along the road, for about 300 metres, proceeding with care. Ignoring the initial left-hand turning, take the main driveway leading up to Woodleaze Farm. Pass through the farmyard, via successive field gates. The driveway morphs into a track as it skirts further farm buildings and passes through further successive gates. Beyond the farm buildings the track curves away to the left, alongside a wall. Continue along the track, to the end of the wall and through the open field that follows until reaching a prominent waymark post.

E The waymark post is incomplete. You need to turn back on yourself, sharp right, at an angle of about 45 degrees, to cross the field in the direction of the woodland. Look out for the gate/stile in the boundary wall ahead, often hidden by the undergrowth. Cross the stile into the woodland and follow the path through it – initially staying near to the field boundary, before gradually descending away from it. Beyond an obvious waymark post continue for about 30 metres, to reach the woodland exit. Take the stile into the extensive, adjacent field. Go left and downhill, keeping within a few metres of the woodland edge until reaching the waymark at its corner. Keep straight ahead and uphill, moving away from the woodland and uphill towards a prominent electricity pylon. Cross the brook and climb towards the waymark post on the skyline ahead. From here, bear slightly left across the field, to take the stile situated about 100 metres distant from the farmhouse. Cross the track and the further stile opposite. In the following field bear right and downhill, to take the stile by the metal gates. Keep on downhill in the same direction, towards the stream. Cross the bridge, as waymarked. Climb the hillside opposite, aiming for the stile in the far boundary fence to the right of the copse. Cross the stile into the extensive field. Initially, keep alongside the left-hand boundary, before (usually) striking up the field in the direction of the electricity pole, by the left-hand corner. This field can be very muddy – conditions may dictate your following all the way around the boundary. In any event, take the gate at the top field corner. In the next field, continue along the left-hand boundary to approach the village of Kingscote. Pass the clump of trees and continue alongside the wall. Cross the stone stile in the left-hand corner. Pick up the driveway ahead and follow it into the centre of the village. Turn left at the T-junction immediately opposite to the church. Proceed along the road for about 100 metres. Take the no-through-road off to the left, signed to Binley Farm and adjacent to woodland. Continue up to the gateway at the end.

F Take the gateway into the parking area, within which you immediately bear right, to exit through the bushes/hedge in the corner. You enter a very long field with panoramic views ahead. Follow along the right-hand boundary wall until reaching the first clear gap in it. Take this and continue in the same direction, with the boundary hedge now on your left. Continue down the field – keeping with the hedge all the way to the bottom corner. Stay with the boundary fence for about 200 metres as it bends around to the right. Cross the stile into the next field. Continue downhill, keeping the fence to your left all the way down to the next field corner. Stay with the boundary edge, as it curves around to the right alongside woodland for about a further 100 metres. Take the footpath leading off

to the left into the copse. Within the copse, take the stile leading into Kingscote Wood proper. As the path morphs into a track gradually descend through the woodland – meandering right and left. Ignore the right-hand turning on the way down, and the further right-hand turning neat to the bottom. Keep ahead, to reach the T-junction with the major crossing track.

G Turn right to follow the track uphill. Keep ahead, as another track merges in from the left and the gradient levels out. Proceed through the field gate in front of the row of cottages. Past the cottages, keep right at the fork, with garages off to the left. Follow the main track uphill as it bends right and left. The track becomes a tarmac lane as you approach the village of Horsley. You arrive at the top of Hartley Bridge Hill, with The Hog pub immediately opposite. From here, turn sharp right towards the main road. Go down Horsley Hill for just over 50 metres before taking Wormwood Hill, a lane off to the right. Descend the steep lane towards the valley bottom, until you reach the turn off to the left, just before the bridge across the stream.

H Turn left on the path, alongside the stream and past cottages. Cross the bridge over the stream towards the clearly signed Mill House. Follow the fenced path around its hedged boundary. At the junction, take the stile leading into the woodland ahead. Proceed gradually uphill with views down towards a millpond. When you reach the crossing path turn left and go along it, to contour along the hillside. Take the stone stile, to exit the woodland into the following field. Proceed, now adjacent to the woodland. Take the gate and keep along the fenced path – still skirting the woodland. Take the next gate. Follow along the narrow ginnel, between gardens. Upon reaching the lane at the end, turn left and downhill for nearly 100 metres. As the lane curves away to the right take the steps down by Spring Cottage, to join the footpath crossing just below. Turn right and keep downhill. Continue alongside the millpond until reaching Ruskin Mill. Exit and bear left along the access road in front of the mill. Exit on to the main road, which you cross straight away. Take the fenced/hedged tarmac footpath immediately opposite to the mill, leading diagonally and steeply up to another road. Turn right and continue for about 50 metres. Pick up the continuation of the same footpath, leading up through scrubland. Upon reaching the road at the top, follow closely alongside the right-hand wall and across the driveway of Rockness House. Take the path down in the right-hand corner. Descend the enclosed path, to reach a further road. Cross to take the fenced/hedged footpath diagonally opposite. As you re-enter the main core of Nailsworth, keep straight ahead across the junction of paths. The path continues past bungalows and merges into the access road ahead. At the T-junction with Newmarket Road, opposite to the Sawyer Hall and Shortwood Chapel, turn right. After about 100 metres, you reach the long-stay car park and shortly thereafter the Chestnut Hill/Old Market junction, where you started the walk. A

No. 20
Wellow, Faulkland and Norton St Philip

Distance 11 miles / 18 kms
Time 5.5 hours
OS Map Explorer 142
Starting Point Village car park, Station Road, Wellow – OS reference 737581
Parking Free car park
Reaching the start from Bristol Go out of Bristol on the A4 towards Bath. Beyond Saltford, at The Globe roundabout, take the road signed for Newton St Loe and Twerton. Proceed through the outer edge of Bath, until reaching the A367 roundabout. Turn right and continue for about three miles, ignoring a couple of minor roads signed for Wellow. On reaching Peasedown St John, continue briefly on the bypass. At the roundabout, just past the Bath Business Park, take the left-hand turn to Wellow. Continue for about two miles until you reach the centre of Wellow. The car park is clearly signed off to the right
Refreshments The George Inn or the Fleur-de-Lys, Norton St Philip; The Faulkland Inn or the Somerset Lavender Farm, Faulkland; the Fox and Badger, Wellow

---

THIS IS A TESTING, undulating walk through the picturesque countryside of north-east Somerset/east Mendip. It encompasses characteristic rolling fields, combes, woods and streams – along with the attractive villages of Wellow, Norton St Philip and Faulkland. Mostly the route follows dry paths and tracks, but there may be some muddy patches.

From the start at Wellow, the walk descends to cross the Wellow Brook and heads up along the valley; soon detouring to a notable Neolithic tomb. The walk continues along the valley towards Littleton Wood. You pass through the woodland and progress across fields to Faulkland. Beyond the village, the route bears eastwards, through fields and along an extended escarpment; with panoramic views into west Wiltshire. After passing several farms, the route turns northwards to Norton St Philip and through its historic village centre. You take an ancient track to the hamlet of Hassage and then climb back uphill again to traverse Baggridge Hill. There follows a circuitous descent back into the Wellow valley. The final section tracks along the valley, back towards Wellow village.

A Go back out of the car park into the main village street. Cross and turn right. Turn right down the path in front of the Fox and Badger public house, Railway Lane. Pass the former steam mill and the former signal box beyond. Continue straight ahead down the walled/hedged path, to reach the Wellow Brook and ford at the valley bottom. Take the old packhorse bridge, to cross the brook. Continue along the road for about 50 metres, and bear right and uphill for about a further 50 metres.

B As the road swings around to the left, keep straight ahead, to take the hedged green lane. Continue for about 400 metres before exiting into the large open field. Keep straight ahead, initially aiming for the hedged corner of the following field. Carry on alongside the left-hand hedgerow and descend towards the gate in the left-hand corner. You can see across to Long Barrow Neolithic earthworks – about 150 metres over to your right and well worth a detour. Return, to take the gate. Head down the next field diagonally, towards the brook and the bottom of the valley. Cross the small tributary and continue, to take the gate in the far corner. In the next field turn sharp left and uphill, keeping with the left-hand hedgerow. Go through the gate into the following field. Keep towards the right-hand hedgerow, past derelict barns on your left. Exit the field in the corner, to pick up the hedged green lane heading towards the corner of the woodland ahead. Stay on this lane, as the right-hand boundary opens up. Continue through two further fields, to reach the crossing track on the woodland's edge.

C Turn left alongside and then into the woodland. Climb steadily on this sunken track and up through the woodland. Just after passing The Knoll on your right, exit on to the road ahead. Turn right and proceed for about 50 metres, before taking the gate off to the right into the field. Head diagonally left, to the top, keeping well to the left of a small building. Continue along the ridge for about 50 metres, before bearing downhill towards the small gate in the far corner by a large oak. Follow the track through the gate and then straight ahead through the hedgerow. Continue on this fenced track – which offers extensive views of the surrounding countryside – for about 1200 metres in all. The first section can be both uneven and muddy. For most of the way, simply keep with the left-hand hedge, initially bending around the edge of three successive fields. As you near Faulkland, the track morphs into a hedged green lane. Continue ahead, to exit on to a minor road. Turn left to reach the main road, opposite to the Faulkland Inn.

D Cross the road, turn left and go downhill. Opposite to the picturesque village green, take the waymarked footpath off to the right through the squeeze-stile. Go past the pond and through another stile, to reach the metalled driveway. (About 30 metres ahead of you is the Somerset Lavender Farm which serves refreshments when open.) To continue on the route: turn left, past the houses and keep left with the driveway as it bends towards garages/stables (ignoring the first right-hand turn). Take the stile/gate next to the stables and enter the field. Continue on the path alongside

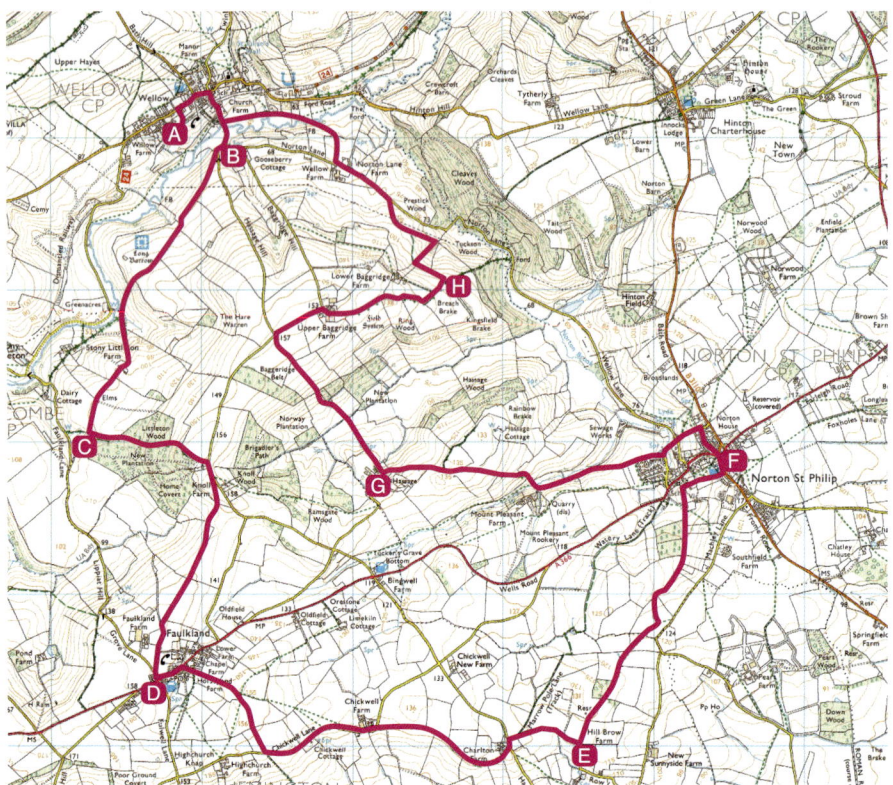

the left-hand boundary, to reach the hedge corner. Climb gently up the field, bearing slightly right and towards the far hedgerow. Look out for the gate in front of a tree. Take this and the following gate, through the hedgerow, into the next field. Proceed along the left-hand hedgerow to exit, via the further gate, into the next field. Head half-right, towards the small gate in the hedgerow, abutting a prominent waymark post. Exit on to the road. (Here you can detour by immediately crossing the road to a secluded seat, hidden away on the opposite side, from which you can quietly enjoy the panoramic views.) To continue on the main route: turn left (right if you have stopped at the seat) and keep ahead on the road, passing several isolated dwellings. Just beyond Chickwell Farm as the road bends sharply left, keep straight ahead up the marked bridleway. Cross another track and continue along this well-defined track for almost 1000 metres in all, as it curves around the hill edge, with further panoramic views. After passing through a field gate, the track descends and becomes more of a hedged/fenced green lane. Go back uphill, through another field gate, to enter a farmyard. Cross the yard to exit on to the road via the further gate. Turn left and pass in front of Charlton Farm. After about 75 metres, take the lane off to the right. Continue along until you reach the sharp right-hand bend, with Hill Brow Farm directly ahead.

E Take the stile to the left of the farm, to enter the field. Cross the field, to take the metal gate in the far boundary. Proceed across the following field in a similar direction, to take the stile on the other side. Keep ahead in the next field, alongside the woodland on your left. Continue to the field corner. Cross another stile and then bear slightly right across the following field towards the further stile in the far hedgerow, just to the right of a tree. Continue on in the same direction up the next field, exiting via the gap into an extensive field, from which you see the village of Norton St Philip ahead. Initially proceed uphill, towards, but not as far as, the trees located in the centre of the field. Bear sharp left and downhill, to take the hidden stile down in the field corner. In the next field, continue alongside the right-hand hedgerow. Exit, via the bridge and stile at the end, into the following field. Keep ahead with the stream on your left. Exit, via the following stile, and straddle along the stream within the hedged track – which extends ahead and morphs into a road as you enter the built-up area of Norton St Philip. Upon reaching the green in front of the parish church of St Philip and St James, turn right and take the gate into the churchyard. Pass the main door of the church and exit through the far gate on to Church Mead – the village recreation field. Head up the field, to exit via the gate in the top left-hand corner. Continue up the path between high stone walls, to exit, via another gate, on to the main village road.

F With the George Inn now on your right and the Fleur-de-Lys opposite, descend and cross Bell Hill. Almost immediately, turn right along North Street. Continue, until you reach the T-junction at the end. Turn left and downhill, passing the triangle of grass at Lyde Green. At the crossroads go straight ahead down Ringwell Lane. Just beyond the left-hand bend turn right, to take the path signed to Hassage and pass in front of Burrgate Cottage. Follow the enclosed green lane, climbing and then steadily descending into scrubland. Go through the gate at the bottom. Continue along the fenced track, as it follows alongside Norton Brook. Soon Mount Pleasant Farm towers above you ahead. In front of the farm, stay on the track, as it bends rightwards towards the brook. Immediately take the left-hand stile into the recently planted woodland and follow the footbridge over the brook. Once over, keep straight ahead to rejoin the main track. Continue steeply up the hedged/fenced track, soon passing various further newly planted woodland. Go through the gate and continue to the top – following up the open field in the same direction, with the hedge on your right. Stay on the track as it passes another hedge, to reach the wall ahead and then bend gently left, alongside it. Pass the ruined farm building on your left. Keep ahead, to reach the junction, with a stony track coming in from the right. Continue downhill on the sunken, hedged track to reach the hamlet of Hassage.

G At the T-junction turn right and continue downhill past the frontage of Hassage House. Beyond the house, go through the field gate and up the hedged

bridleway. Keep along the bridleway, gradually descending to cross the stream. As the surfaced track ends, turn left into the field. Immediately turn sharp right and continue steeply uphill alongside the right-hand hedge – in the same general direction as before. Continue all the way to the top of the field, where you follow the track, through the copse and up into the next field. Turn left, within the field, for about 50 metres – before turning sharp right to follow the uphill track. Take the gate in the far hedgerow into the following field, and continue uphill in the same direction. Exit via the field gate on to the crossing road. Turn right in the direction of Baggridge Farm – obvious ahead – with panoramic views both left and right. As you reach the farm the road bends sharp left. Go straight ahead on the byway and through the farm complex. Keep on down the fenced track for about 800 metres in all. Soon ignore a private driveway, off to the left. Likewise ignore a public footpath/driveway, off to Lower Baggridge Farm, much further down. Beyond this, continue for a further 100 metres until reaching two adjacent gates off to your left.

H Take the first of the two field gates. Follow the right-hand hedge of the field, down to its corner. Go through the gate, across the small field and through another gate into the extensive field that follows. Turn right and keep alongside the right-hand edge. Beyond the first corner, continue along the fence in the direction of the far right-hand field corner. Before you reach the field end, take the gate into the adjacent field, down to your right. Continue in the same direction as before, with the same fence now on your left. Upon reaching the field corner, bear diagonally right and down the field, to take the gateway in the hedgerow leading on to the crossing road below. Turn left down the road, towards Wellow. After a total of about 400 metres, and about 75 metres beyond Norton Lane Farm, take the gate off to the right. Continue down the left-hand hedgerow. Take the gate, to enter the following field. Bear sharp left down towards the gate halfway in the boundary fence. Continue diagonally downhill on the alignment of the church spire, towards the field corner in the valley bottom. Take the gate/footbridge/gate over the stream. Keep straight ahead, to join the crossing track. Turn left along this track, to take the field gate into an equestrian centre-cum-timber yard. Pass through this complex and exit via the further field gate. Continue straight ahead along the valley, passing through the next field, to take the further gate ahead. In the following field keep straight ahead, all the way along the right-hand boundary. At the far corner exit via the gate on to the road, immediately opposite to the packhorse bridge you crossed early in the walk. Head towards the bridge, to rejoin the path you walked down earlier. Turn right, to retrace your steps uphill and re-emerge next to the Fox and Badger pub. Turn left along the village street and back to the car park where you started. **A**

No. 21
Wedmore, Rodney Stoke and Nyland

Distance 9 miles / 15 kms
Time 4 to 4.5 hours
OS Map Explorer 141
Starting Point Public car park off Worthington Close, Wedmore – OS reference 437482
Parking Free car park
Reaching the start from Bristol Go south on the A38. Continue past Bristol Airport and through Churchill and Sidcot. Turn left to take the A371 signed to Wells. On reaching Cheddar, keep with A371 for nearly a mile, then turn right on the B3151 signed to Wedmore. On reaching Wedmore, look out for the signs to the car park – off to the left, before you reach the centre of the village
Refreshments The Swan or other facilities in the centre of Wedmore – at the start or the finish of the walk

---

THIS IS A MAINLY EASY walk, exploring the peaceful rhynes, moors and meadows of the Somerset Levels to the north and east of the historic village of Wedmore. The ascent to the top of Nyland Hill provides a spectacular overview of the surrounding area. The walk follows mainly tracks and lanes; but includes a couple of muddy stretches during the winter months. A good walk for spotting wildlife.

The walk starts at Wedmore, which is well worth exploring in its own right, before or after. You set out eastwards across Wedmore Moor to pick up the River Axe, which you follow alongside through several fields. The route diverts off via a track/lane towards Rodney Stoke. From the village church, you bear in the direction of Nyland Hill, through various farms, Draycott Moor and the fringes of Draycott village. There follows the, at first gradual but eventually steep, ascent of Nyland Hill, rewarded by 360-degree views over the Levels and beyond. You descend to follow Nyland Drove across further moorland and over the River Axe again, to reach the hamlet of Cocklake. The walk concludes with an attractive stretch back to Wedmore along an ancient track/path.

A From the car park take the pedestrian signs towards Wedmore village centre, to reach the secondary car park access, the T-junction at Worthington Close. (If you want to visit the village centre before or after the walk, as I would strongly recommend, turn right here.) To start the walk, turn left. The road immediately morphs into a green lane beside a stream/rhyne. You soon emerge out of the village on to the Somerset Levels. Nyland Hill is visible over to the left and the Mendip Hills straight ahead. The track becomes raised, with the stream/rhyne to the left and the ditch/hedge on the right, with trees regularly interspersed. Keep straight ahead. Take the stile, cross the joining rhyne and go through successive field gates. Proceed on the now hedged track, crossing a further rhyne, to reach a field gate ahead. Go straight through and into the following field. Keep ahead parallel with the right-hand boundary, to take the similar footbridge over the ditch. In the next field bear very slightly right, to take a similar footbridge over the further ditch on the far boundary. In the following field continue, hedge left, with a backcloth of farm buildings behind the line of trees in the far boundary. Take successive stiles through the trees, to join the path running alongside the River Axe. Turn right, to take the footbridge across the river.

B Over the footbridge, turn right along the riverbank. Often there are distant views of Glastonbury Tor directly ahead. Follow the riverbank through ten fields in all. The river curves away to the left, as you pass mostly through gates. In the course of the eighth field, a substantial solar farm materialises over on the opposite bank. Keep ahead, pass a waymark post and through two further fields until reaching the field gate opposite to the solar farm's furthest extent.

C Do not go through this gate. Instead, take the waymarked path off to the left, to follow alongside the lesser, joining rhyne. Aim towards the field gate ahead, with the distant backdrop of the Mendip Hills. Take this gate into the next field. Continue in the same direction, still alongside the rhyne. Cross the stile by the following field gate, after which the path morphs into a green lane. As you pass Treasures Farm and various farm buildings further along, the lane becomes tarmacked. Keep ahead, passing Lower Stoke Farm on the left. Ultimately, you reach a T-junction. Turn right along the road and immediately cross the bridge over a disused railway. Follow the road around to St Leonard's church, Rodney Stoke. Take the stone stile into the churchyard, where there are several well-placed seats. Proceed through the churchyard, to exit via the main church gate. Cross the road.

D Take the stone stile. Go straight down the field and through the gate. Go half-right across the next field, to take the stone stile just to the left of the stand of beech trees. Cross the following field diagonally, aiming for the white house. Exit in the corner, via the field gate. Turn right along the road, passing Honeyhurst Farm and crossing the rhyne, to reach the T-junction ahead. Turn left along Brook Bank – the road signed towards Wedmore. After about 300 metres turn right down the no-through road. This soon

becomes a poorly surfaced lane, with ditches on either side. Continue straight ahead until, about 50 metres before the left bend, you take the stile on the right next to the field gate. Enter the adjacent field and go half-right across it, avoiding the boggiest patches as best you can. Cross the footbridge in the far right-hand corner, over a rhyne. In the following field, turn left alongside the rhyne and bend with it, until reaching the stile/footbridge/stile, by an electricity pole. Cross the rhyne and bear slightly left along the next field. Take the gate near the left-hand corner leading out on to the lane, by the sewage works. Turn left along the hedged lane/track, pass Dolmead Farm and proceed to the T-junction ahead. Turn left and follow the road over the rhyne (Dolmead Rhyne, which you crossed earlier). Keep uphill as the road bends right and passes through Batts Farm and other farm complexes, to reach the junction in front of Crate Farmhouse.

E Take the left-hand track, towards Rookery Farm. The track bends to the right and passes through the farm. Take field gate ahead, as the track becomes hedged and climbs the hillside beyond. Take the further field gate, to access the open land within the Nyland Hill perimeter. Proceed into the field for about 100 metres, beyond which you strike out up the open hillside towards the fenced tree. From the tree, climb up the hillside more steeply. There is no well-defined path but you keep broadly

parallel with the boundary of the woodland over to your right. Climb on up until reaching the trig point at the summit. There are fine views over the Somerset Levels. Nyland Hill once belonged to Glastonbury Abbey. In the pre-Norman period, when it was surrounded by marshland, it is thought to have had a chapel and probably a hermitage. Descend in a westerly direction, on an alignment towards the extensive group of farm buildings situated immediately below. Head down on the sometimes steep and eventually obvious path – aiming towards the field gate at the corner of the bottom hedgerow, which forms the perimeter edge. Pick up the crossing track at the boundary, turn right and immediately take the gate. Follow the track down the next field, hedge right. Exit, via the stile, on to the road beyond adjacent to Quay Farm and opposite to Tor Farm.

F Turn left along the minor road, Nyland Drove. Follow around the bend. Cross the bridge over the substantial Hixham Rhyne. Continue ahead to the T-junction to reach the River Axe once again. Turn right along the more major road, immediately taking the bridge over the river. Continue on the road, for at least a further 500 metres; to reach the edge of the hamlet of Cocklake. Upon crossing the bridge over a further rhyne, proceed for about a further 150 metres, to reach Yew Tree Farm on your right.

G Immediately opposite to the farm, take the turning off to the left. Continue along the lane/track, as it curves around to the right. Immediately before Crate Farm, take the track off to the left. Keep straight ahead on the green lane, soon passing through the first gate. Exit at the end, via the following gate, into the adjacent field. Continue on the path via five fields, crossing various gaps, stiles, bridges and gates. At the end of the fifth field, go through the hedgerow to pick up the track, which you continue to follow along the right-hand edge of three more fields. Upon passing through the field gate at the end of the third field, the track morphs into a hedged lane. As the tarmacked lane bends sharply around to the right, take the field gate immediately ahead and into the adjacent field. Wedmore church is visible ahead, over to the right. Cross the field diagonally, to the far right-hand corner. Exit via the gate into next field. Keep uphill, along the left-hand boundary hedge. Within about 100 metres, take the stile leading into the car park access road. From here, return to your vehicle. A

No. 22

Wells, Croscombe and Dinder

Distance 7.5 miles / 12 kms

Time 3.5 hours

OS Map Explorer 141

Starting Point Outside the west door of Wells Cathedral – OS reference 553458

Parking Various long-term parking in or near to the centre of Wells – mostly charged

Reaching the start from Bristol Go out of Bristol on the A37. Just beyond Farrington Gurney, leave the A37 and continue straight ahead on the A39. Continue on, through Chewton Mendip and beyond, eventually reaching the centre of Wells

Refreshments The George Inn, Croscombe; or plenty of options in Wells. One seat above Croscombe with panoramic views, suitable for picnics in the right weather

---

AN ENJOYABLE CIRCLE taking in the magnificent city of Wells, the high ridge to its east, two traditional Somerset villages and the attractive countryside around. The walk is mainly on footpaths, through fields and woods. The terrain is mostly easy, with a couple of short climbs.

The walk starts at Wells Cathedral. You pass the Bishop's Palace before climbing Tor Hill and proceeding eastwards along the ridge/plateau, through woodland and fields. You descend, via an ancient track, to the village of Croscombe. The route returns westwards along the valley, to the village of Dinder, and through open fields, back towards Wells. There are scenic vistas of the city, in particular the cathedral, as you approach. The opportunity to explore the city more fully after the walk should not be missed.

🅐 With your back to the west door of Wells Cathedral, turn left on the paved path along Cathedral Green. Go through the small arch, the Penniless Porch, and into the Market Place. Almost immediately turn left, through the arched entrance and into the Bishop's Palace complex. Turn right, to follow the path alongside the moat. At the first corner, turn left with the moat. Keep ahead all the way along the path, to exit through the barrier on to the road ahead. Cross, and take the gated lane almost immediately opposite. Proceed for about 50 metres, to reach the footpath signed off to the right and leading into woodland.

🅑 Take the footpath. Climb up the steps and uphill through Tor Hill Woods. Ignore all side paths, to take the gate at the top. Enter the open field beyond and continue straight along it. You soon enter woodland again. Follow the waymarked path, as it meanders and leads, via the next gate, into open land again. Keep straight ahead along the first, narrow stretch of the field. Then, follow the right-hand boundary fence of the disused quarry and woodland, as it bends away to the right. In the far corner the field narrows into a track, which you follow along into the next field. Turn left and down the centre of the narrow field. At the end cross the stone stile and turn left, up the crossing track. After passing the farm on your left, the track climbs alongside the golf course and then through it. Keep ahead as the track evolves into more of a footpath and climbs gently along the edge of King's Castle Wood – a nature reserve/ancient wood. With the golf course on your right, follow the waymarked path all the way along until it curves left, to enter

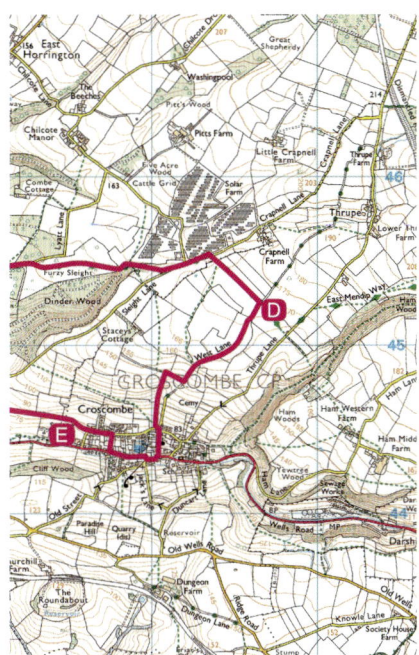

over to the right. Pick up the track in the far right-hand corner and follow it through the gate, beyond which you drop down into the hollow. Keep straight ahead and parallel with the line of trees (ignoring the sharp right-hand fork up the embankment). Gently climb the embankment straight ahead. Continue through the following field. Take the gate leading out on to the lane ahead. Turn left along the lane, for about 300 metres. Just before a telegraph pole and opposite to the solar farm, turn right and over the signposted stile in the hedgerow. Bear slightly left across the narrow field, to take the triple stile. Keep ahead up and along the centre of the next field. Take the stone stile in the end hedgerow, to join the crossing track.

the woodland. Proceed uphill and take the gate. Continue to climb as the path meanders more steeply uphill. At the top, you exit the woodland into the adjacent field to join the crossing track.

C Turn right along the track. Proceed through the large open plateau surrounded by woodland, keeping towards the left-hand boundary. Take the short passage through the woodland ahead. At the end, take the field gate into open land again. Initially keep adjacent to the left-hand woodland and then follow the field boundary, to reach the very far end of the long field. Take the gate and proceed along the bounded lane/track through woodland, for about 150 metres. Take the right-hand gate through the hedgerow and into the following field. Keep left and follow diagonally the full length of the field, passing a brick pillbox

D Turn right along the enclosed, ancient track of West Lane. Proceed for about 500 metres. As the track begins to descend and views of Croscombe open up over to the left, another path joins in from the right. Keep ahead downhill, for about a further 100 metres beyond. Just past the double field gate, turn right along the narrower hedged path. Continue for about 100 metres, until reaching the stile in the left-hand hedge. Cross the stile, beyond which there is a welcome seat with views of Croscombe below and across Somerset beyond. Proceed straight ahead down the field and through the gate in the hedgerow. Continue down, towards the gate/stile in the bottom left-hand corner of the field below. Exit on to Fayreway, the road bounding the northern edge of Croscombe. Turn left and then immediately right down Church Street. You pass St Mary's church on your left, and soon

meet the old Market Cross at the main road ahead. Turn right along the road. Within about 100 metres you reach The George Inn. To continue: carry on in the same direction for about a further 300 metres. Immediately beyond Elderwell House take the alley leading up to the right, to rejoin Fayreway. Turn left and continue until reaching the post box and seat, at the first bend.

E Take the adjacent stile/gate into the field. Go up the field and through the gate in the hedgerow ahead. Continue up and along the valley side, through the next field. The gate in the corner takes you into the following field. Maintain direction, keeping to the left-hand hedge, now going downhill. You can see Dinder ahead and Wells beyond. Take the gate and cross the lane. Follow the path, straight through the field gate opposite and across the next field. Take the further field gate into the succeeding field, which is often very muddy. Advance along the fenced track to reach the curtilage of Higher Farm, from which you continue in the same direction. Take the field gate, off to the right into the field and then turn immediately left. Proceed ahead, to go over the stone stile, across in the far boundary. Continue straight across the following field, to exit via the gate out on to the lane. Turn left down the lane into the centre of Dinder. Turn right at the T-junction, to soon pass the fifteenth-century Church of St Michael. Carry on straight ahead via the left-hand fork in the road. You reach the recreation ground, which you access via the main gate. Follow the grassy track around the right-hand edge, to take the gate by the pavilion. Head to the far right-hand corner of the next field and through the gate. Proceed along the right-hand hedgerow of the following field. Just before the boundary kinks left, turn right and through the small gate, over a bridge and into the adjacent field. Continue left along the hedgerow. At the first field corner turn right, to continue up the hedgerow. Ignore the

130

gateway entrance to the next field. Rather, follow the hedgerow around the next field corner and continue along the bottom hedgerow of the field. Take the gate in the far left-hand corner and cross the subsequent field, bearing just to the left of the oak tree. Take the gate and cross the track. Take the similar gate into the field beyond and follow the left-hand hedgerow. Further panoramic views open up towards Glastonbury Tor, and you pass a further pillbox. Enter the next field via another gate and bear left across it. Exit, via the next gate, on to the road. Cross the road and take the footpath opposite, to reach the crossing track, with a gate ahead of you.

F Turn left down the hedged track – rather than the more obvious tarmac path straight ahead towards Wells. The selected route is more scenic and less used. Continue for about 300 metres until you reach the crossing path. Turn right, to take the stile through the hedgerow. Bear slightly leftwards, up the field. Aim towards the protruding, right-hand corner of Park Wood. From this corner, advance along the edge of the woodland, to take the stile into the next field. The city of Wells and Wells Cathedral in particular, become increasingly prominent ahead. Continue along the edge of the woodland to the next corner – from where the Monarch's Way emerges and joins. You now follow the Monarch's Way along the left-hand hedgerow, via the gate and through the park all the way into Wells. Exit via successive gates, to reach the southern corner of the Bishop's Palace moat, which you followed earlier in the walk. Retrace your earlier steps along the moat, through Market Place and back to the starting point at Wells Cathedral. **A**

Do not miss the opportunity to explore Wells further. There is plenty of interest in and around the cathedral precinct. Vicars' Close, a group of 14th-century almshouses, is reportedly the oldest purely residential street in Europe with its original buildings still standing.

No. 23

Coaley Peak, Selsley Common and Woodchester Park

Distance 8.5 miles / 14 kms

Time 4 hours

OS Map Explorer 168

Starting Point Coaley Peak Car Park – OS reference 794013

Parking Free parking in Coaley Peak car park

Reaching the start from Bristol Go north on the M5. Exit by Junction 13 and turn right to take the A419 towards Stonehouse. At the first roundabout, turn right towards Eastington and proceed through the centre of the village. At the roundabout turn left, to go through Frocester village. At the top of the steep Frocester Hill (in wintry conditions it may be advisable to seek out a different route), turn left along the B4066. The car park is off to the left after half-a-mile.

Refreshments None – but numerous seats with panoramic views suitable for picnics in the right weather conditions on Selsley Common and in Woodchester Park

---

THIS UNDULATING WALK traverses the wooded slopes along the western escarpment of the Cotswolds; Selsley Common, with its open panoramic vistas across the Severn Vale; and the secluded, landscaped valley of Woodchester Park, incorporating an incomplete Gothic mansion. The route follows well-defined tracks and footpaths.

The walk starts at the viewing-point on Coaley Peak. After soon passing Nympsfield Long Barrow, you contour the ancient beech forests of Stanley Wood and Pen Wood. There is then a climb up to Selsley Common, from which there are spectacular panoramic views – as far as the Sugar Loaf and Hay Bluff on a clear day. The route turns southwards across the Common, up to Bown Hill and down through a vineyard. Upon reaching the bottom of the Woodchester Valley, you follow the driveway into the National Trust estate, proceeding all the way through the wooded/landscaped grounds set along a series of lakes. After passing the allegedly haunted Woodchester Mansion, you ascend out of the estate to the head of the valley, to soon return to the Coaley Peak car park.

A From the car park head across to the viewing area on the edge of the escarpment, to enjoy the spectacular panoramic views stretching across the Severn Vale and Severn Estuary. To start the walk: turn right and along the escarpment. You soon pass Nympsfield Long Barrow, which is 5,500 years old, and certainly worth a stop. Proceed down the waymarked path, to approach the woodland over in the right-hand corner. Continue through the gate, which defines the official perimeter of Stanley Wood, managed by the Woodland Trust. Within the woodland, the key principle is to closely follow the frequent yellow Cotswold Way waymarks. The path initially runs alongside the road. About 50 metres beyond the official entrance, bear left and down the short flight of steps. Cross another track, to take the gate ahead. Continue gently uphill for about 50 metres, still near to the road. Bear left, to pass through the further gate. Continue along the waymarked path, as it gradually bends away from the road and broadens out. Descend gently down the escarpment, passing through a succession of wooden barriers. Towards (but not at) the bottom, exit the woodland, via the gate, into the following field. Proceed on the path/track along the top edge, threading between trees on the fringe of the woodland. As the track emerges fully out into the open, advance into the following field. Cross the field and take the stile into the following one. Pass the farm complex down to the left, as you proceed, to take the next stile back into Stanley Wood.

B Back within the woodland, proceed along the track for about 100 metres. At the junction, keep right with the Cotswold Way – bear up the embankment and continue uphill. Past the Woodland Trust waymark, the track levels out and contours the hillside through the wood. At the fork in the tracks, keep left and downhill with the Cotswold Way. Continue to contour the hillside of Pen Hill for at least a further 1500 metres, until reaching the edge of the village of Middleyard. After descend-

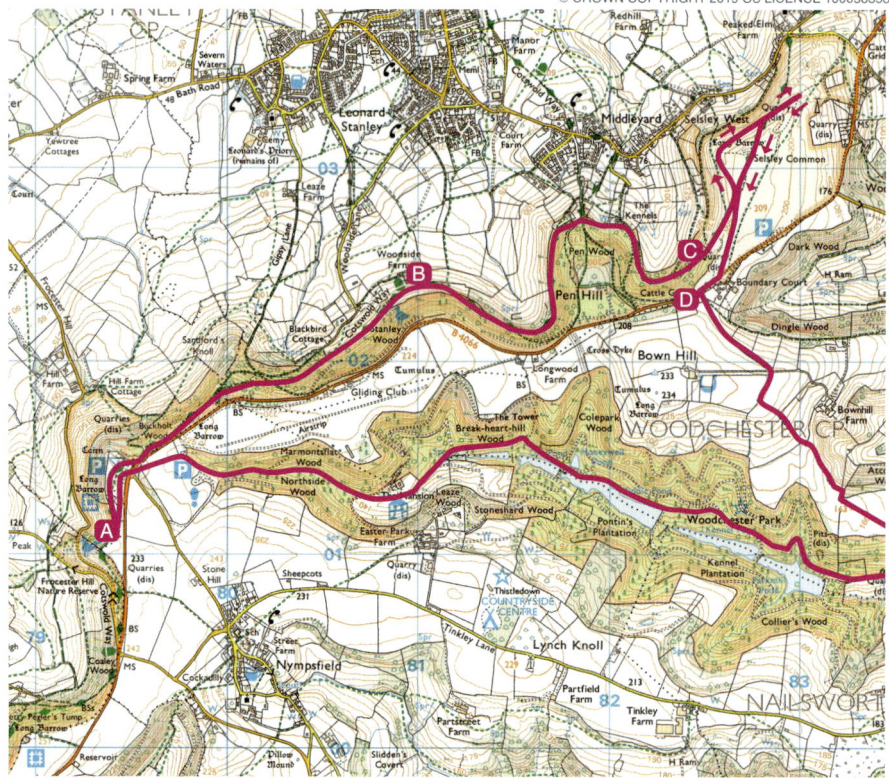

ing the short flight of steps, you reach a further major path junction, at which the Cotswold Way divides. Take the path peeling right - signed Cotswold Way North via Selsley Common - via the gate immediately ahead. Keep left and downhill via further steps, as the path progresses in close proximity to the edge of the woods. Take the stile, after which another path merges from the left and the path widens. Go straight across the private access road and through the barrier. Continue straight ahead, within the woodland and along the now broad track. The track soon bends sharply around to the left. About 150 metres beyond, take the right-hand fork. Proceed up the hillside on this steep track, to reach the gate at the top.

C Exit the woodland, via the gate, on to the open grassland of Selsley Common. Go forward, through a group of bushes, and follow the waymarked path uphill, passing the former quarry, over to your right. Climb up straight ahead to the top of the hill, from which there are spectacular views. There are a plethora of well-positioned seats. Once on the hilltop, you immediately reach a waymark post - about 50 metres beyond which, turn left, to take the major crossing path along the ridge. Head towards the left-hand edge of the prehistoric tumulus, known locally as the Toots and labelled as Long Barrow on OS maps. At the tumulus turn right, to follow around and along its far side. Pass (for now) the small topograph and continue along the ridge (ignoring the Cotswold Way fork going

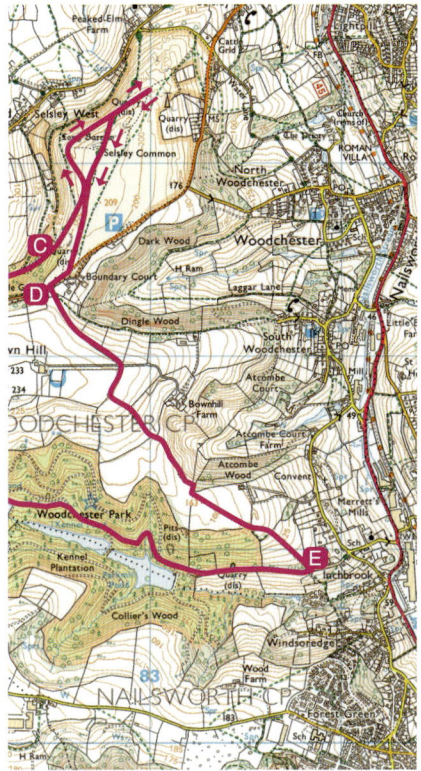

down towards the village of Selsley). There are more disused quarry workings over to your right, and scenic views towards Selsley church down to your left. Upon reaching the seat at the far end of the quarry workings, turn right and continue their circumnavigation. Come back upon yourself, to return to the topograph you passed earlier, from which you can now take your bearings. Strike out in a south-westerly direction towards the distant complex of buildings, Boundary Court, fronted by the B4066. Pick up the well-defined path heading in this general direction. At the multiple junction of paths keep straight ahead – still aiming for the distant buildings and staying on the higher ground. The path passes several seats. Keep straight ahead and near to the woodland on your right, eventually reaching a small parking area, opposite to Boundary Court. Cross the road and turn right, along the verge and in front of the property.

D At the main gateway leading into the adjacent Bownhill Farm estate, take the footpath signed to Woodchester. Proceed up the surfaced driveway through the avenue of trees. After about 400 metres, at the multiple junction of tracks, go straight ahead through the stile/gate (ignoring the turn off to the right signed towards the Livery). Continue along the enclosed track next to the drystone wall. After about 100 metres, take the left-hand metal gate, into the adjacent field. Follow the left-hand boundary all the way down, to take the stile leading into the next field. Continue down and back up the long left-hand boundary, to reach the stile on the left towards the far end of the field. Take the stone stile and immediately the tall gate, to enter a vineyard. Follow the path diagonally down the field on the line of electricity poles. Go through the hedgerow. Continue downhill, initially just within the right-hand boundary but then being careful to follow the circuitous waymarked route. Meander left, before taking the stile through the further hedge and continuing downhill in a straight-line, through the rows of vines. Exit the vineyard in the bottom right-hand corner, via the further tall gate. Proceed downhill through scrubland, to join the crossing track at the bottom.

E Turn right along the crossing track. Immediately go through the gateway, to enter the National Trust's Woodchester Estate. Continue along this driveway through woodland for at least 1500 metres, ignoring side turns. A series of lakes down to the left become increasingly obvious through trees. When you

reach the first junction of equal tracks (although only the route ahead is waymarked), take the left-hand track downhill and towards the lakes. At the bottom the track curves right and follows beside the lakes. At the corner of the lake ahead, take the waymarked path immediately alongside. At the end of this lake, you come to a T-junction ahead. Turn left and downhill on the crossing track, past the small lake over to your right. Continue ahead, past the boathouse on another lake down to your left. Follow straight ahead alongside the next lake. Continue through the gate, to reach the end of the lake. Climb the steps up the embankment, to rejoin the driveway you were on earlier. Turn left and pass along the driveway, through various gates and towards Woodchester Mansion. It is well worth arranging a visit, though you must check the opening hours in advance. Past the mansion, keep ahead along the fenced driveway. Go through further gates and up towards the head of the valley. Beyond the fenced section, continue on up through the woodland. Pass the gatehouse on your right and emerge through open land. Keep along the driveway until reaching the main gate. Exit the estate via the stile to the left of the main gate, leading out on to the B4066. Cross the road at the junction. Go straight ahead, through the small gate immediately opposite and into scrubland. Immediately bear left with the path and follow it through the woodland for about 50 metres. Turn left to reconnect with the Cotswold Way. Retrace your footsteps in the direction of Coaley Peak car park, from where you started the walk. **A**

No. 24
Chew Magna, Stanton Drew and Pensford

Distance 10.5 miles / 17 kms
Time 5 hours
OS Map Explorer 155
Starting Point Entrance to St Andrew's Church, South Parade, High Street, Chew Magna – OS reference 576632
Parking Free parking in the village car park behind the Pelican Inn; or towards the east end of the High Street, Chew Magna
Reaching the start from Bristol Go south on the A38. Continue for two miles, beyond the outer ring road. Shortly beyond the traffic lights at the right-hand B3130 turn, take the left-hand B3130 turn, signed to Chew Magna. Proceed for four miles to reach Chew Magna. Continue to the end of the High Street, near to the church
Refreshments Druid Arms, Stanton Drew; Rising Sun, Pensford; Carpenters Arms, Stanton Wick; various options in Chew Magna

---

THIS WALK takes in a long section of the Chew Valley – encompassing many panoramic views and the quintessential villages of Chew Magna, Stanford Drew, Pensford and Stanford Wick. The terrain of the first half is mainly level, but the second half is more undulating. The route is principally along easy tracks and footpaths. A couple of sections, however, can become overgrown during the summer months and require long trousers.

The walk starts in the centre of Chew Magna and follows the river eastwards to Stanford Drew. After passing the Stone Circles, you continue alongside the river and under the spectacular viaduct to reach Pensford. After crossing the A37 you keep on through Publow to reach the edge of Woollard. At this point the route turns southwards and westwards along a well-defined track/driveway/lane to re-cross the A37. You continue through woodland and then climb to Stanton Wick. The walk traverses various farmholdings and fields, before a steep climb up Knowle Hill, from which there are spectacular views, including of Chew Valley Lake. The final section starts along the ancient track of Pitts Lane, which eventually leads you across the river again and back to the centre of Chew Magna.

A Enter St Andrew's churchyard, via the main entrance from South Parade. Proceed on the main path past the ancient cross. Just beyond the church door, bear right along the tarmac path by the wall. Exit the churchyard and continue ahead on the drive, bearing around to the right and past the main entrance to Chew Court. Keep left along the avenue of trees edged with mossy stones, passing the cricket field. Exit via the stile, to cross the B3130. Take the gate opposite and follow along the left-hand hedge of the field, to take the gate in the far-left corner. Cross the bridge over the River Chew – the first of several crossings during the walk. Take the next gate and continue along the hedged track. Fork left on the lesser path, to briefly continue beside the river. Climb gently up into the field ahead. Follow around the boundary towards the farm building – just to the right of which, take the gate into the next field. Follow the downhill path, towards the group of pines in the valley. Take the gate and the footbridge, to join the crossing track. Turn right and stay on this hedged green lane as it bends and undulates. Keep ahead for a total of about 1000 metres, to reach the edge of Stanton Drew. The track morphs into Sandy Lane, which you stay on until it joins the main road in the village centre. (The Druid Arms public house is a small detour, about 100 metres along to the right.)

B From the junction, the main route continues left and along the main road for about 50 metres. Turn right and uphill, alongside the triangular green. At the top turn right again, alongside

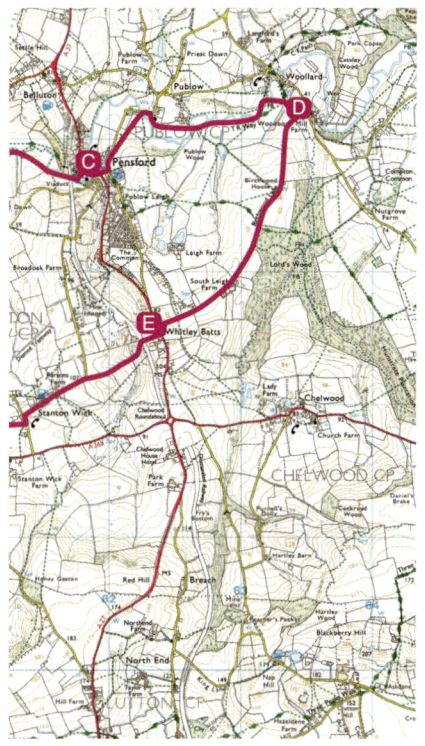

the outer wall of Stanton Drew Court. (Almost immediately you reach a sign off to the left for the Stone Circles – to visit them, detour here.) To continue: keep straight ahead through the gate and along the metalled farm driveway, passing the church and the Church Farm complex. Continue through the next gate. Keep with the driveway as it bends, passing the main stone circles in the field immediately to your left. Go through the small gate, situated between the two field gates, to leave the driveway. Strike out down the field, keeping broadly parallel with the driveway and aiming to the right of the copse in the near distance. Take the gateway in the hedgerow at the bottom and into the following field. Bear slightly right, passing just to the left of a power pole, to exit via the gate in the hedgerow ahead.

In the next field continue ahead, aiming to the far left of the row of trees, before bending slightly right to exit, via the gate, out on to the lane ahead. Cross the lane. Go up the short track and through the following gate. Keep towards the left-hand hedge, along the field and towards the gate leading back out on to the lane. Exit, to re-cross the lane and take the gate into the field opposite. Follow the left-hand boundary hedge and take the small gate – next to the field gates – into the following field. Keep along the river through three meadows/gates until exiting, via the gate, adjacent to the bridge at Byemills. Go straight ahead on the track with the stone house on your left, to take the field gate ahead. Still alongside the river, continue through the overgrown meadow. Proceed through the gate and gently uphill on the narrow, fenced path. Climb the steps and take the further gate. Enter the large field that follows and head down it in the direction of the Pensford viaduct. Take the footbridge and the gate. Continue along the fenced path, with the river again on your immediate left. Take the next gate, go under the railway viaduct and keep left to cross the scenic bridge over the river. Skirt Pensford church as you pass though the car park of the Rising Sun and out on to the road. Turn right along the road, cross the river again over another scenic bridge, to reach the crossroads with the A37.

C Cross the A37 to take the road straight ahead signed to Publow. You soon reach, in close proximity, the ancient well and the seat dedicated to local musician Acker Bilk. The main route continues off to the left, along Publow Lane. Continue up the right-hand footpath for about 100 metres and follow it, past iron railings, through the gate and into the field. Keep ahead along the field, near to the left-hand hedgerow. Take the gate

into the following field, as the fine tower of Publow church appears ahead. Bear slightly right and downhill, in the general direction of the church. Take the next gate and continue down this field to exit via the gate on to the road – over to the left of the church. Turn right along the road and over the bridge. Before the church, turn right on the railed path between the churchyard and the River Chew. Take the gate into the following field. Keep adjacent with the churchyard boundary as it bends away to the left. Advance in the same direction, pass the farm buildings and pick up the farm track. Continue through the gate and across the river again. Take the gate immediately ahead. Proceed on the farm track, through two fields and two gates, with the river meandering alongside. Continue through the following field, within which the track morphs into a path. Go through another gate. In the next field, keep alongside the river for about a further 100 metres until reaching the crossing path emerging from the bridge over the river. Turn sharp right to take this path across the field towards woodland, aiming for the gate just to the right of derelict industrial buildings. Take the gate/footbridge, to join the tree-lined track.

D Turn right and climb steadily uphill. As you pass the farm on your left, the track morphs into a metalled driveway and gradually levels out. Beyond the entrances to Lord's Wood, the driveway further morphs into Birchwood Lane. You pass another farm over to the left, and a further one over to the right. Keep along the undulating lane, eventually climbing towards the busy A37 at Whitley Batts. Cross the A37 again and look for the footpath opposite, adjacent to Pensford House.

E Descend the hedged/fenced ginnel between houses and gardens, across the route of the old railway line and into woodland via the gate. Within the woodland, continue downhill. As the path curves leftwards to the valley floor, follow alongside the stream and then cross it

via the wooden bridge. Climb straight ahead, to exit the woodland in the right-hand corner through the gate. Enter the field and continue uphill next to the right-hand hedgerow. Continue through the gate and stay alongside the hedgerow all the way up the next field. In the top corner, take the gate, to exit on to the road. Turn left along the road and soon reach the hamlet of Stanton Wick. Pass Parsons Farm, beyond which is the Carpenter Arms. Continue along the road to its junction with Stanton Drew Lane, adjacent to the small green. Keep left for 50 metres or so, until reaching the footpath sign. Turn right, to take the footpath in front of the row of cottages. Go through the gate into the field. Bear right down the field, keeping towards the right-hand hedge and on an alignment towards the buildings of Stanton Drew, spread out in the distance below. Go through the gate in the hedge. Carry on down the next field in a similar direction, aiming for the right-hand hedge corner and then following the right-hand hedge. Take the further gate and keep on down this narrow field. Exit via the gate in the hedgerow ahead. In the next field, descend the left-hand hedge to the corner. Cross the stream, via the gate/footbridge/gate, into the following field and immediately turn left along the boundary, for about 75 metres. Turn left, to take the bridge and steps into the woodland. Curve around to the right with the path, within the perimeter of the woodland. Exit, via the gate, into the following field, within which you keep ahead alongside the right hedge. Go straight ahead through the gap in the corner and into the next field. Keep ahead along the left-hand boundary, skirting the buildings of Bromley Farm. At the field end, turn sharp right with the field boundary. After about a further 75 metres exit left, via the gate in the hedgerow. Follow the right-hand hedge through the next field. Exit on to the lane next to the farm entrance. Turn right along the lane for about 30 metres, looking for the footpath in the left-hand hedgerow.

F Take the gate into the field. Initially keep with the right-hand boundary. Then bear slightly left, to take the gate in the hedgerow ahead and enter the curtilage of Curl's Farm. Follow the right-hand fence through the paddock, to cross the drive via successive field gates. Pass across the front of the main house. Bear left down the next paddock, towards its left-hand corner. Take the gate and keep along the left-hand hedge, within the further paddock. Exit by the next gate on to the track. Turn left through the gateway into the large field. Immediately deviate from the track to continue in the same general direction. At first, follow the right-hand hedgerow, to skirt the small knoll immediately ahead. Then keep ahead, to ascend the larger hill beyond. Take the gate into Curl's Wood, situated on the earthworks of an ancient fort. Follow the track through the trees and maintain direction to exit via the gate. Cross the lane, take the steps immediately opposite and go through the gate. Continue straight ahead down the fenced path, next to the large paddock area. Keep downhill, to cross the small stream and take the gate into the following field. Climb quite steeply, alongside the left-hand hedgerow, towards the crossing road at the top. Exit, via the gate, on to the road.

G Immediately opposite, at the start of Hollowbrook Lane, climb the steps on the right and take the gate into the field. Bear left, along the field, towards the waymark post in the near corner, aiming just to the right of a power pole – your precise route will depend on whether the field is cropped or not. From the (sometimes obscured) waymark, follow the footpath along the right-hand hedge for a further 100 metres or so. Take the footpath, down to the right, through the gate in the hedgerow and into the adjacent field. Stay alongside the hedgerow and cross the small field towards a large oak. Take the gate into the wooded/

scrubby area. Keep left and then bend right and uphill; to cross the lane edging Knowle Hill. Follow the footpath on to the bracken-covered hillside. After no more than 5 metres fork right, to divert on to the lesser path. This path can become overgrown in the summer months but, with persistence should always prove passable. Follow the path as it curves up and around the hill, to eventually reach a major crossing path. At the T-junction, turn left and climb steeply up on to the ridge, from which there are 360-degree panoramic views of the Chew Valley and, in particular, Chew Valley Lake. You reach a prominent seat, from which you continue ahead along the ridge. At the fork, at the end of the ridge, take the path that bends left and downhill. Maintain direction, through the bracken and across several crossing and joining paths, to reach the far perimeter hedge of Knowle Hill with Chew Magna Lake directly beyond. Turn right within the hedgerow and stay alongside it. Descend towards the obvious house and take the narrow, enclosed path running down to its left. Exit the path, via the gate, into the adjacent field. Proceed down the right-hand edge and past two recently built houses. Join the driveway and keep straight ahead as it morphs into the ancient track – Pitts Lane – which you follow for at least a further 800 metres. After passing the farm on the right, continue through the gate ahead, beyond which the track becomes more of a wooded path. Descend gradually, to reach the crossing lane.

H Go over the lane and climb the steps/fenced path, up the opposite embankment. At the top, take the left-hand gate into the adjacent field. Head down the right-hand hedgerow and through the gateway into the next field. As you near Chew Magna again, bear diagonally left down the large field, past a power pole. Take the gate down in the far left-hand corner, to reach the track by Dumpers Cottage. Turn right, for about 50 metres. Turn left at the junction and go across the wooden footbridge. Continue through scrubby woodland. Cross the stone bridge and then go immediately right along the path, initially by the river. This soon becomes a walled/hedged path climbing uphill. Pass through the barrier, to reach Chew Magna High Street again. Cross the road and turn right along the raised pavement, passing several fine old houses, to return to the start. **A**

Some reaction to *Beyond Bristol: 24 Country Walks*

Excellent – the walks are of a good length and very well described.

Walks suitable for everyone. Excellent, especially if you are not familiar with the area and enjoy trying new and interesting walks.

We have enjoyed every walk made even more sociable by a fab choice of pubs. Your instructions are spot on ...

Really well-written directions – surprisingly rare in walking guide books ... What a great book!

Brilliant walks with great maps.

Well-written, good walks, good maps and attractive photos.

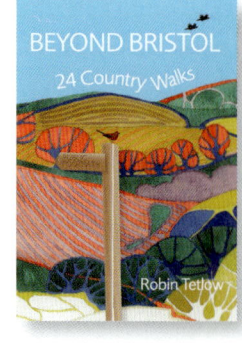

Lara Tetlow

Robin Tetlow was born and brought up in the Midlands and lived in various parts of the UK, before eventually settling in Bristol. He co-founded Tetlow King Planning Ltd, a town planning consultancy specialising in housing, in 1985. Robin has had a lifelong interest in walking, travel and the natural environment. Following on from *Beyond Bristol: 24 Country Walks* (Redcliffe Press Ltd, 2017), this is his second compendium of favourite walks in the countryside around Bristol, based on more than 30 years of exploring the area.
www.beyondbristolwalks.co.uk

 beyondbristolwalks